Advance Praise for
Beautiful Monster

"Magic realism is, thankfully, still alive, and Miles Borrero uses his literary lineage to tell the compelling story of his own becoming. In *Beautiful Monster*, he artfully describes the ubiquitous anxiety, like Poe's thumping heart under the floorboards, that comes from hiding one's true self from his loved ones, from the world, and most poignantly—from his own culture. It's a gift to be shepherded through this process with such deftness, humor, and pathos."

—**Alexandra Auder**, author of *Don't Call Me Home*

"An enthralling read, beautifully written, that offers an insider's view into the inner workings of growing up queer and trans in a straight world. Simply a must-read."

—**Cameron Esposito**, standup comic, bestselling author

"Miles Borrero gifts us his universal story with grace and a huge, lyrical heart. A roadmap for anyone seeking self-knowledge."

—**Ty Burrell**, award-winning actor who starred in ABC's critically acclaimed hit *Modern Family*

"Miles' storytelling shows us just how intricately the mundane and the divine are connected. Through his poetry and prose, Miles harnesses a transformative power—a power that brings his deepest truths to the light. This memoir is a gift to any reader who wants to truly know themselves, and wants to truly be known."

—**Lauren Patten**, Tony and Grammy Award winning actor and singer (*Jagged Little Pill*)

"Spell-bound from the first page to the last, I laughed, cried, and deeply resonated with every twist and turn in this expansive and magical tale. Miles Borrero truly touched my heart."

—**Stephanie Szostak**, actress (*A Million Little Things*) and author of *Self!sh*

"*Beautiful Monster* is like a big, queer hug. Exactly what the world needs."

—**Kathryn Budig**, author and founder of Haus of Phoenix

BEAUTIFUL MONSTER

A Becoming

MILES BORRERO

A REGALO PRESS BOOK

ISBN: 979-8-88845-000-0
ISBN (eBook): 979-8-88845-001-7

Cover design by Howard Grossman
Cover doodles by Milo Rubin
Cover photo by Carlos Borrero
Interior design and composition by Greg Johnson, Textbook Perfect

This is a work of memoir. The events are portrayed to the best of the author's memory. While all the stories in this book are true, some names and identifying details have been changed to protect the privacy of the people involved.

Regalo Press
New York • Nashville
regalopress.com

Published in the United States of America
1 2 3 4 5 6 7 8 9 10

A Mami & Papi,
for instilling the deep,
unflinching sense of worth and belonging
that has allowed for this extraordinary journey
toward unearthing my center.

To Tío,
for showing me where the magic lies.

And to all the trancestors
and younger-than-me gender nonconformist originals,
for your bravery and unstoppable imagination.
You are the true measure of a whole heart.
May the world realize this someday soon.

Author's Note

This memoir is a true re-membering. An act of stitching myself together by piecing fragments of family folklore with bits from my life and spinning them into something new, something whole. In these pages, I attempt to describe my past experiences with as much honesty as possible, though I've also heightened certain moments with magical realism, understanding that these stories are not solely mine. My aim is not to write in absolute truths, but rather to offer the reader an intimate glimpse into how these moments were *felt*. Where present-day insights have occurred, I have allowed them to shine forth, fleshing out events, offering them dimensionality in the process of catalyzing my own healing.

My ancestors' names have been preserved in honor of their memory and contribution. Most other names have been changed for privacy. At times, people, events and places have been blended, as my wish was never to point to any specific person, but rather to study with curiosity how my becoming has intersected with theirs.

I also wish to acknowledge that, while each trans person's journey is unique, the overall experience of walking this path reveals challenges and gifts that are worthy of exploration by both the reader and the world at large. My wish is to invite you into the depth of feeling, wisdom, and magic that we bring to the table.

I.

Phasing In

Marina

"Sweetheart, if you're waiting for your parents to die in order to do what you need to in this life, I'm afraid you'll be waiting a very long time," Ferguson, my partner, offers unprompted as we get ready for bed.

I hope she will stop speaking.

She's right, of course. I know this, as I sit on the toilet of our tiny Brooklyn bathroom in inconsolable tatters. My father has been in the hospital for four weeks. It is now clear that he is dying. I haven't slept well in years, and my crippling worry and anxiety have gotten unbearable of late.

"Your dad won't be around much longer, but your mother's people live forever. She might outlive you," she says, not unkindly.

Her directness sucks the air right out of my lungs.

"It's better to dive in sooner than later. Otherwise you may not get to do it at all." Done flossing, she glances at me through light blue eyes. Her words burn. And not entirely in a bad way. In a cold plunge, wake-me-up kind of way I can't even be mad at her for.

We slide into bed, where she falls asleep midsentence thanks to her brain meds, while I lay there envious that she can sleep like that. She's out cold. Snoring in uneven, maddening flurries without a care in the world, twitching, and nabbing me occasionally with her pointy elbow. Our two tiny dogs snuggle into her: Arlo, the Chihuahua—self-appointed back-of-the-knee warmer—and Hank, the Maltese—the feather-soft equivalent of a hot water bottle right at tummy level. Leaving me alone to stare at the shadows on the ceiling and think. About Death, mostly. And home.

I grew up in Colombia, South America, home to world-famous coffee, Shakira, and yes—cocaine. Which, along with our national treasures—Fernando Botero, the painter and sculptor of Rubenesque figures, and Gabriel García Márquez, the father of magical realism—made for a world brimming with contradiction and paradox.

The Colombia I was raised in was bludgeoned by war. A war that spared no one. Pablo Escobar's Colombia. Where fear spread faster than lice and we responded in kind, lighting the streets on fire with the smoky, sultry *taca-taa taca-taa taca-taa* of our feet hitting the pavement to the rhythm of salsa music. The harsh taste of aguardiente, our local liquor, fresh in our mouths, offering false courage for that singular moment in time, singeing our throats with anise.

By the time I left Colombia to attend college in the US, I'd seen as many deaths on my parents' TV as strangely wholesome black-and-white reruns of *Leave It to Beaver* dubbed in Spanish. Every night, piles of lifeless bodies in mass graves filled the screen. Mostly campesinos (field workers) in far-off towns, those who've always paid others' debts in our country.

Then, the most infamous death of them all—Escobar's—replaced our despair with shock and surprise in 1993. The photos of his limp body crumpled facedown on the red tiles of a rooftop, surrounded by smiling soldiers, etched themselves into the backs of my eyelids in a way I would never unsee.

Though my family was lucky enough to be spared from the cartel's immediate violence, we did suffer our fair share of family deaths over the years. On Dad's side, his parents, Abuelo Ernesto and Abuelita Marina, and on Mom's, her beloved older sister, Tía Cris.

I'd seen enough to appreciate that Death doesn't look the same on everyone. Which is fascinating, heartbreaking, and, if I'm honest...a bit exhilarating. But not when I think about Dad's. When I think about his death, I hit a panic wall of nothingness. I freeze. I can't see beyond the moment my own life will shatter.

———

Headlights pierced the darkness, as Moby Dick—the great blue whale of a car—came to a full stop at the edge of the flooded road ahead. Hail the size of mothballs pounded the roof.

"Mila, wake up! I need you to go out there and see if we can make it through the puddle." Mom craned her neck to look back at me, distressed. I bolted upright, yellow beret dangling awkwardly atop my bowl cut. My hand ripped it out of the way mechanically, without much thought, like I did when I was little—chunk of hair and all. I'd fallen asleep in the back seat after horseback riding with the car's easy sway. No longer able to curl up on the floor like I used to—enveloped by the warm hum of the engine, inhaling the faint fumes of gasoline. Still drowsy, I polished the foggy window with the sleeve of my sweater, making it worse as I peered out. We were still on the dirt road on the outskirts of Bogotá and were running late to Abuelito Ernesto's funeral. The puddle was more like a small pond, and the road was deserted.

Slipping off Susie's old penny loafers, I exchanged them for my rubber riding boots. The sensation of pantyhose against the stiffness of the boot made my skin crawl. All family members have roles, and I knew mine. Mine was to do the "get dirty, wet, and cold" jobs, and I kind of loved it. I grabbed the tiny umbrella (which at our house was always the faintest suggestion of one) and stepped out into the tempest. Wading through the muddy water, I looked back. Mom offered encouragement from the crack in the window, a goldfish coming up for air: "Go on, honey! I'll follow you!"

My boots sank deeper into the mud, a tear in the left one letting the sludge seep in slowly as I searched for the shallowest path. Mom and Susie trailed behind me, oscillating in my wake. I hoped we wouldn't drown the motor. If we did, our luck would be out, and here, on this solitary dirt road near the stables, there was no way to send word. I kept treading, focusing on the dry land ahead. The water now a third of the way up the car door, my foot sloshed inside my boot as I towed the *Titanic* behind me—the smallest of tugboats.

When we made it through to the other side, I climbed back in, relieved.

"Thanks, honey! You're such a trooper."

At church, Abuelito Ernesto's coffin was displayed starkly at the center of the altar, dripping in white garlands. I knew he was in there, but it didn't feel real. The cathedral, impersonal with granite floors and vaulted ceilings, was freezing. My damp foot, a block of ice. The priest waved incense over the coffin muttering under his breath. I watched the ritual with apprehension. I felt numb. Dad's grief-stricken face exposed the weight of our loss.

When we went to stand by Abuelita Marina at the end of the service, she examined me, sour-faced, lips turned down as if she'd been sucking on a lime. Her eyes landed on my dirty foot, making her growl in a low decibel only I could hear, "What young lady shows up to her grandfather's funeral looking like a filthy animal?" I stared at my guilty feet with shame, cheeks flushed by the glare of her rage, saying nothing. Not yet knowing that the shame I felt was actually hers, not mine. Not yet knowing that I would be much happier as the animal I am than trying to turn myself into a lady.

That was the last time I saw her, Marina, standing on her own two feet.

It was also one of two times I remember seeing Dad at church. The second—when he was front and center.

That same night. The night we buried Abuelito Ernesto—who died from the same lung condition that would eventually kill Dad— Marina did something of Marquezian proportions. That night, she crawled into Abuelo's empty hospital bed in the bedroom of their Zen-style home, never to climb out. Until we buried her ten years later. Transforming his bed into her coffin.

A romantic might mistake this with the dealings of a broken heart, and though that was surely part of it, it was much more than that. Marina, one of the first women in Colombia to drive a motorcar, who carried a ladylike (yet still deadly) pistol in her purse, had been wild and unruly when she was younger, but something essential had hardened over time. Making her mean in her old age. Lifelong resentments turned her into a kind of female Don Corleone—unflinching, absolute, and impossibly possessive.

Don't get me wrong: her anger was a fixture. Family lore had it that, on the day of the Bogotazo, the 1948 riots, Marina fought her way through the uproar to look for my then seven-year-old father. Jorge Eliécer Gaitán, a liberal poised to win the heated presidential election, had minutes before been assassinated while delivering a stirring speech in a central plaza in Bogotá, unleashing the unprecedented disturbance. In the heat of the moment, church-run schools attempted to remove themselves from politics altogether by releasing their students, my dad among them, into the streets without warning and closing their sanctimonious doors behind them.

When my grandmother made it to the plaza, where people frantically clawed at Gaitán's body trying to snag a bloody keepsake, she spotted Dad instantly—jaw dropped and wide-eyed. Dragging him out of the mob by his collar, she furiously listed off (as Colombians say) "what he would die from"—ignoring that it could be her own chokehold. Breezing past the lollipop-shaped tree in the driveway, the pink rotary phone in the foyer, and the oasis of plants in the knitting room, she whipped Abuelo Ernesto's belt off the valet stand, using it to beat him raw. Neither of them knew why.

So Marina's temper ran caliente, to say the least. Coming from money, she was a small-town princess, entitled and used to getting her way. Which, in her youth, made her wildly captivating. A streak of unbreakable fierceness Ernesto couldn't find within himself. A kind of proof of life he didn't possess. He was a steady, solemn man. He needed that spark almost as much as sunlight. So he whistled every morning, while drinking his tinto, his black coffee, at the tiendita across the street from her window. Like a lovebird hoping to draw her out. His mating call, eventually wearing her haughtiness down, giving her an unfamiliar, almost uncomfortable settled feeling. Something she'd never felt before but liked. His clear gray eyes then sealed the deal.

She fell in love with his quiet mystery. Too much in love perhaps. He balanced her, made her fire bearable, and she adored him for it. Disarmed by it all, she agreed to marry him, despite his younger age and humble beginnings. Something she never forgave herself for. Their age gap was no small humiliation and was not to be mentioned by anyone, ever. We never knew exactly how many years she had on him, since each time she renewed her driver's license, she managed to convince the clerk to dock a couple more years off the prior age by slipping him a nice stack of bills. Leaving her with IDs ages eighty-one, eighty-five, and eighty-nine by the time she died.

Love failed to make up the difference between her head and her heart over the years, leaving her with the acidic feeling deep in her gut that Ernesto had not been good enough for her in the end. And now that he was gone, now that he had left her alone with no one to torment, her anger crystallized into the shocking, stubborn decision to lie there calcifying into a fossil right in front of our very eyes.

———

Ferguson and I met on an app. When I saw her picture, I knew we would be together. Call it fate. Or a feeling. After some preliminary flirting, we moved things off the app, texting back and forth. And though things seemed to flow, she wouldn't agree to go out with me. For months. Like eight of them. But I didn't give up. I'd text her from time to time, asking what she was up to. Until the whole thing had gone on long enough and I was done.

I wrote her one last time. "Hi, we've been texting for eight months and I think you're swell. But this is the last time I'll ask you out. And I have to say, I think you're making a mistake if you don't go out with me." The response came back immediately. "Are you free this Friday?"

I learned later that she'd somehow, in those eight months, "acquired a girlfriend," as she put it. Who she abruptly un-acquired prior to our first date. I asked her to dinner at my favorite Argentinian restaurant in Williamsburg. I was locking my helmet onto my motorcycle and giving my hair one last zhuzh in the side mirror when she showed up looking perfectly understated in white skinny jeans with pink loafers, red hair shining in the afternoon sunlight. We were seated in the back patio with lots of twinkly lights and a romantic ambiance. Everything, idyllic. We talked about her acting work, growing up in the South, her life in the city...and then the focus came to me.

"So, you're a yoga teacher?" she asked, already knowing the answer.

"Yup."

"And you live in Bushwick?"

"That's right." Our texts had been pretty bare bones.

"But not, like, in one of those firetrap lofts with nine people and five cats?"

I had to be honest. "Well, actually..."

"But your roommates don't make kombucha in the bathtub?" she teased.

"Well...actually...one of my roommates does have a gnarly-looking scoby in our fridge for that very purpose." Her cheeks turned bright red. She laughed. I laughed too, self-conscious. The particulars of my living situation often worked as a device to separate the wheat from the chaff.

I felt like it was either the best date I'd ever been on or the worst. And for the life of me, I couldn't figure out which. Luckily, she was my kind of people and decided to stick around.

Lying in bed paralyzed by the black hole of Dad's impending death, my mind has nowhere else to go but her words. Ferguson is right. *I have been waiting.*

I'd started using the name Miles socially, in my New York life, right before we met. It'd been a vulnerable transition for me, and one that most of my friends, yoga students, and employers chose to ignore. But Ferguson jumped right in from day one, unapologetically insistent on reminding people to use my name. The one I had chosen. The one I wanted to be called. She was so charming that no one could resist her. Since we'd been together, I'd also changed my pronouns from she/her to he/him, where once again, she'd been pivotal in helping others bridge that gap.

The dam breaks. Tears stream down my face. I am so unequivocally Latin in this. The *way* I cry. Big and unstoppable. Almost comical.

The truth, the real truth, is that I've been so terrified of hurting my parents that I have been biding my time. All these years, I've thought naively that I could protect them. All these years, I've felt guilty. For leaving Colombia, moving to the States. Guilty for making space between us without knowing why. For choosing myself, my freedom. I've even felt guilty for continually chipping away at unlearning the shame I've carried about who I am. What I am. Even if I don't understand exactly what that is yet. Shame that was never mine to begin with but was ingested as frequently as coffee and is as jagged as the feeling after too many cups. I've been so terrified of hurting my parents that I am literally doing that which most pains me—hesitating, pausing, stalling. Waiting is not the same as living. I know something must give, even if just a little. For a ship that has changed course by the smallest degree ends up at a completely different destination.

Camila

On a balmy São Paolo morning, an eerie silence befell a sterile hospital room. Stillness hung in the air for an infinite second, a caesura, a gasp. The Ancients, gaze drawn to the horizon, awaited the inevitable: the very moment—though Time is a slippery and ever-changing thing—when dimensions would converge. Time nauseatingly stretched herself out like taffy...and just like that...

Waaaaaaaaaaaaaaaaaaa!

My newborn wail—and first song—bounced off the walls, slamming the room along with all those in it back into the forward motion of existence. I was birthed.

My shriek muffled yet another sound underscoring the chaos. An electric crackle, a white noise that rumbled through the spirit world, imperceptible to human ears. Out in the fields, horses sniffed at the air, whipping their tails impatiently. Fluttering exhales of mist through tapioca lips. They could smell the snag in the fabric of Time.

I broke Time as we know it.

Well, *I* didn't break it. The deeper, more ancient part of me did. The me that has always been, has never changed and never will, because it cannot be affected by Time or circumstance. That part. It had a different idea of what was to pass and, being Time-less, had more clout.

Anyway, I guess it doesn't matter *why* it broke. It just did. The system. The code. The compact. Or contract. Whatever you want to call the unspoken universal law set forth by the order of things. Nobody meant for it to happen. But it did.

My spirit bifurcates. Though not entirely. Two halves of a whole split, yet overlap in the present moment; the penumbra in my eclipse—darkness dissolving into light. Or is it the other way around? Leaving me stuck, perhaps forever, between worlds. Though not in the way you might think. This gray, viscous state of becoming will grant me permissions others dare not dream of. Allowing me to glide seamlessly between worlds, unfettered by Newtonian restrictions, in sync with the chaos and uncertainty of the quantum realm of Time and Space—which are expressions of the same thing. Gifts such as these are reserved for the few because only we sense them and unlock them, out of necessity. My gift will lie awkwardly dormant for many years. Waiting for me to catch up to the reality of its existence. Making itself known in seemingly insignificant ways, while Time chips away at me, offering up more questions than answers. Eventually, though, I will learn that I can slow Time down, and also fold her onto herself, overlap her—live several Lives at once.

In this beginning, though, Time simply refused to follow her usual structures around me. Meddling with even the smallest, most mundane attempts at joining this realm, like a name, or a birthday. And with a sharp sense of humor I found frustrating, she also made a point to ruin all watches and electronics I came into contact with, making them go berserk, flashing their lights or staying their hands. Making me feel like she didn't want me here, like she'd never intended for me to get through the snag. Until I began to realize, much later, decades later, that she was rigged in my favor. It turns out she had been calling for me all along. Sending those signs to lead my awareness to my gift. Asking. No! Demanding that I remember: it, me, what could be.

> *In the world that was water,*
> *truth was thick*
> *Like the bellows of Time.*
> *Like silence—*
> *sound inverted.*

———

My arrival, the crowning event of our stay in Brazil, set into motion our family's imminent move to Venezuela. My family, Colombian by birthright, had already moved around Central and South America for Dad's work during the first era of my parents' marriage. Happily, they landed in Brazil. It was my infant war cry that ended their sunny, friend-filled, nine-year tenure in the magical land of samba, beaches, and warm-blooded people who spoke in sloshy Portuguese that dribbled all over your senses and stuck to you like fresh pineapple juice, making you drunk with pleasure. Our furniture, well on its way to Caracas, made me the last unyielding piece refusing to fall obediently into place.

First, there was the question of my name.

And names are a serious question.

My parents wanted to call me Mila, already made infamous by a Brazilian porn star in the late '70s. Not wanting to saddle me with ill repute, they settled for Camila, and called me Mila anyway.

There was a second impasse, more stubborn than the first. One pertaining to clan and country. In Colombia, a person has two last names: the father's, followed by the mother's maiden name—in that order. Together, the two comprise one's last name.

In Brazil, it's backwards. The child's first last name is the *mother's* maiden name, with the father's last name appearing as a sad second. My sister, four and a half years older, was already Susana Borrero Echeverry, with Dad's last name parading front and center like a peacock. Making it hard for my parents to explain a newborn with the name Camila Echeverry Borrero (even if Mom did do all the work of producing me out of her very tiny body). What would people think? Nope. It simply wouldn't do. It was a question of clarity, nothing more. If a child comes out of a woman but doesn't have the man's last name, does the child even exist?

But because I broke the system, my not-yet-legal existence further delayed our move to Caracas because Dad couldn't find a way to fill out my registration forms without ending up with someone else's baby—namely Mom's. How could it be so hard to name a baby anyway?

He took his pleas to the Colombian consulate, where things played out like a good ol' telenovela. There he sat, in the clerk's office [*worried music swelling*]...sweating profusely into his button-down [*pan to the moisture on his upper lip*], day in and day out, bringing the clerk coffee and pastries, asking if there was any other way to file paperwork yielding a child clearly belonging to him—a proper child. The answer always the same. No. [*Close-up of eyeballs darting left and right.*] No amount of coffee or sugar cookies would change that.

Yet, he persisted.

Every morning, the events repeated with little to no variation. After two weeks of this, one morning, a solution occurred to the clerk. She was a nice person after all and wanted this for him as much as he did, mostly because, well, she wanted him out of her office. She waved him up to the counter. "Don Carlos, have you considered filing Camila's registration with *only* your last name on it?"

Dad leaned in, examining her with an eagle eye. "I can do that?"

"Yes, I believe it's been done before. It isn't ideal, but they'll accept it. You'd be filing as if you were a single dad. Camila just won't legally have a mother to speak of. On paper, that is."

Sweat dribbled down the sides of his face. He had been due in Venezuela weeks ago! No need to consult Mom or anything; she wouldn't mind, would she?

"Let's do it!"

And with a decisive wave of his pen, I forever became: Camila Borrero _____.

On paper, a motherless child—with a loving, living mother. And already quite the rare Colombian citizen, as it was unheard of to have only one last name.

With that, Dad unknowingly pointed me toward my fate, though really it was more like a destiny: a stamp of approval on a preexisting condition of illegitimacy from the universe that would linger throughout my whole life.

The next impasse sealed the deal, though.

"There's only one more thing," the clerk announced.

My father squinted at her. This sounded bad. "What's that?"

"You're past the grace period for filing Camila's registration. I'm going to have to fine you."

[*Eyeballs widen.*] Dad, averse to paying any and all fines, and well versed in the art of making them disappear, pleaded, "Ay, senhora, o que eu vou fazer? Is there no way around this? I'd be so grateful

16

if you could help me. You see, I'm expected in Venezuela for a new job and have already stayed past my allotted time. Você compreende, na? Moving a whole family to a new country along with a newborn..." He flashed her pathetic long-lashed eyes with eyebrows drawn high on his forehead.

She caved. "Well...there is *one* way around it. You could...change her birthday to *today*?!?!" Lowering her voice, confiding in him, "I'm not supposed to do this. But considering the circumstances, I think I can make an exception." She crinkled her nose and slid the forms under the glass.

[*The record scratches as everything lurches forward.*]

In this moment, a shearing force organizes the chaos into a divine order different from what was. Making unseen things fully expressed while others shift into ghostlike, paper-thin expressions of themselves. It's a volatile place, the world of nebulous space inside the big bang. Existence doesn't come without risks. And there's always a dab of the unaccounted for that sneaks into the mix. The magic. Things happen along the way that shift even the Universe's plans sometimes, ever so slightly.

"Muito obrigado!!!"

And just like that: one mother short and birthed twice—but only once on paper—within two weeks of this life, I was finally deemed fit to join this realm, having complied fully, though messily, with its natural laws.

Inconsistencies would continue to surface throughout my life, though, like wrinkles on a shirt—my own reincarnation in action.

And so it was that I wound up living several lives at once in one lifetime. Why wait until Death? I don't have that kind of time.

Now, finally, everything *appeared* normal. Except it wasn't. Or was it? Who's to say what *normal* feels or looks like? Who's to say normal is even a thing worth aspiring to? That's the thing about karma. We weave ourselves into it without fully appreciating what we are doing. My father's choice to course-correct may have been a logical one, but the Universe cares little for logic. Energy doesn't suddenly die or disappear—it *transforms*.

Hanuman

Hanuman stands flanked by his army on the Indian mainland, hands on his hips. Bewildered, he gazes over the expansive waters at the Isle of Lanka. So far away. The glare of the sun making his small monkey silhouette visible while casting a shadow painting him a giant on the sand.

He is desperate to help Rama, his best friend, save his beloved Princess Sita from Ravana's evil claws. The rakshasa has abducted her and is holding her hostage in Lanka.

Gazing across the twinkling kaleidoscopic waters, he feels so small, so helpless. All he ever wanted was to be of service to Rama, he loves him so. Though they've been hard at work building a bridge, there is no way they will be able to move their armies across the ocean in time.

Just as he reaches the pit of his despair, the wind surges around him, making ripples in the water. He hears a whisper. His father, the Wind, murmurs in his ear.

Hanuman, remember...
Remember who you are.

You are my son.
Son of the Wind!

REMEMBER.

He has forgotten himself, forgotten he is the son of Vayu—the Wind God.

REMEMBER.

The memory, locked inside him for so long, is suddenly jogged free. Remembering, his gifts bubble to the surface, superpowers that they are. He begins to grow and grow, bigger and bigger, growing to ten times his size. Alive with the extent of his power, he sprints toward the water's edge springing with all his might into the air, surprising even himself. One leg outstretched in front; the other, like a rudder, in the back. The wind swooping him far off the ground, swelling, howling around him like a tornado, carrying him into flight. Sweeping him across the tides, all the way to Lanka.

Remember...

Re-Member...

Put yourself back together again. Or for the first time. Ever.

———

Before I could even walk I was gifted my first horse. A Fisher-Price gelding with yellow reins and stylish cherry-red seat for a saddle. I named him Alazan—Spanish for brown, even though he was spotted black and white. Proof of my budding sense of humor. He made my first getaway ride—freedom in hot blue wheels—and the gateway to many other rides I would enjoy throughout my life: skateboards, bicycles, motorcycles, boats, surfboards, snowboards...my breath.

In Caracas, the three-story house came with three long flights of steps. One morning, I pulled on a pair of green lederhosen Marina and Ernesto had brought back from Austria, instead of the customary doll dresses Mom dressed me in. A die-hard Snoopy fan, ready to end the Red Baron, I conjured his cool from deep within my soul as I nudged my mount to the lip of the top step. Pulling swim goggles over my eyes, I surveyed the landing. The only sound now, that of my breath. I listened.

So Hum

Hearing it consciously for the first time. The sound of my breath. Like a secret I didn't know was there. A little seed—a bija—a syllable, an utterance. The sound Tibetans have translated to I *am that*. The most essential mantra of them all. The one we are born with and cannot live without, our soundtrack and companion until we die. The song of our very spirit.

So Hum
I am that

Looking over the edge, I knew nothing to be truer.

With everything stilled, the gooey substance of Time slowed to match my rhythm, becoming languorous. Space came into focus, visible to me now. Expanding. I could see through the dimensions as surely as someone looking up at the night sky might fall into the creaminess of the Milky Way. And I was not alone. *They* were here too. It was the first time I remember feeling them. The only one I recognized was Peris, Mom's grandma. Who, in life, lost her vision to a coal iron exploding in her face, leaving her with a glass eye, almost entirely blind. She had to go to Europe by boat to try to save the last few shadows she could see. Mom always told me she watched over me. She was right. There were also others I didn't recognize, fanning around me, hands on my shoulders as we peered over the ledge together. I took another breath.

So Hum

It ricocheted against the banks of my insides, so simple, so obvious, syncopated against the beat of my heart, assuring the success of my venture, or so I figured. With my battle fist tearing through the air, and my other hand steady on the reins, I kicked off the ledge with a loud,

AHHHHHHHHHHHHHHH!
Thunk
Thunk
Thunk
Thunk
Thunk

Rifling my way down to the bottom. Mom, hearing the racket from the kitchen a little too late, ran in holding her chest, stopping the heart attack. Landing at her feet I laughed hysterically, looking up, tearing the goggles off my head, elated. The Ancients, still up top, peered down. Speechless. Witnesses, not judges. Their language, that of winds and whispers.

"Camila, what did you do?!?!"

And just like that, I snapped back into the room.

———

Caracas was short-lived.

Abuelito Ernesto had amassed a small fortune working in the coffee business in Bogotá. With it, he purchased a restaurant and a small rose farm on the outskirts of the city, enlisting Dad and Tío Gus to work with him, turning the flowers into the family business.

Maybe Dad was tired of working for other people, though I can't imagine that being the case. Latin American executives had it pretty plush back in the late '70s and early '80s. In Brazil, his office was furnished with a cook and fluffy towels for post ocean swims. Hour-and-a-half lunches gave them enough time to go to Ipanema, come back, shower, and finish the rest of the workday by five. And in Venezuela, while ACES Airlines flew him all over the world to appraise airplanes, we enjoyed a glorious little house in a secluded enclave with a tight-knit group of friends, all with kids around the same age. Life was wonderful.

Or maybe he had no choice. Maybe Marina made the call: "Son, come home," the phone going dead before he could respond, lest he forget his place. Long-distance calls were horrendously expensive and either way, she wasn't asking. His parents were, after all, the quiet kind of scary.

Merlin

My folks tried everything they could to exhaust me physically. I had A LOT of energy. Around the age of four came swim lessons, which I hated. The pool, more like a polar bear dip in the frigid Bogotá air, was over-chlorinated to the point of burning my little nose hairs right off. Latins don't care for guidelines, instruction manuals, or reading signs for that matter. And we are as fastidious as they come. Which is why we don't see a problem with adding a double dose of chlorine to kill off anything still living in the water, including the people swimming in it. There was also the too-tight swim cap that Colombians insist be worn in all pools, so tight it gave me a headache. And to top it off, the floors in the locker room were scuzzy—the wafting fumes of Fabuloso singeing my eyelashes—with nasty hairballs in the drains.

Tennis followed, which I loved. The smell of felt and fresh rubber when I cracked the lid off a new canister of balls was intoxicating. As well as all the things I could do with the balls once I gained dexterity. I was starting to derive great satisfaction from exploring my motor skills and seeing them improve and develop as my body learned to move through space in ways that were demanding, graceful, and made me light on my feet. I loved the crisp whack the racket made when striking the ball and my swift, sharp exhale—*HUA*—that came with it and was purged out by the force of the impact. Courts reeked of the sweet funk of sweat, and the sound my sneakers made while sliding on the red clay was thrilling.

Some days the caddie would even let me push the large powdered sugar sifter of chalk, retracing the old court lines with new shimmery ones. I found this task soothing—combined simplicity and purpose. A walking meditation. The chalk, with an evocative clean, crisp smell of its own, still delights me to this day when sniffing my fingers after a good rock climb.

And finally, on weekends, Mom tacked horseback riding lessons onto everything for good measure. After tennis, Susie and I scrambled into the back of Moby Dick and changed into our breeches while she drove to the stables, an hour away. ABBA, Mom's all-time favorite (which, to this day, can turn even the most rancid mood in our house into a sunny one in the space of a hot Swedish pop measure), blared from the cassette player to Susie's favorite song, "When I Kissed the Teacher," as we all belted it out at the top of our lungs. We were well versed in the whole ABBA canon, not just their greatest hits. Susie, who would've probably been happier staying home reading or writing in her diary, was dragged on all aforementioned adventures by virtue of my existence.

The stables, a glorious place that smelled of oil, horse dung, sawdust, leather, and fresh-cut grass, were full of magnificent pockets to explore and nooks to get lost in. All kinds of tools were lying around, to cut grass, for upkeep, cleaning the stalls, and making horseshoes. It was an earthy place where freedom was measured in quantities of dirt, and Susie and I took to it immediately. I also appreciated that the teacher, Patricia, who was in her twenties, didn't mind calling me Daniel-san (a.k.a. the Karate Kid) and wasn't fazed by the yellow bandana I insisted on wearing even over my helmet.

Riding quickly became the family favorite.

If you're a horse person, you know. You know! The smell of horses alone makes people crazy. They are magnificent creatures. And the art of riding is a profound study in the yamas and niyamas, the yogic proposals for right living in relationship to others as well as to one's self. As horse and rider come together, a nuanced connection is initiated, the centerpiece of which is respect. Meeting and being met, that's the practice. But it only works when both parties are able to hold their own integrity within the relationship—interdependence. In riding, as in life, there are excellent matches and horrible ones, as well as everything in between. It's impossible to hide the truth of our essential nature in the naked space between horse and rider. They can smell us, what we're made of. And the distance between is then negotiated through a kind of drawing back in on our animal senses, where we are given the chance to relearn embodied communication. Through touch, smell, listening, presence, and even taste. Because when you get that metallic taste of fear in your mouth, you'd better pay attention.

Years later, when I dive deeper into my studies of yoga, I come across one of Patanjali's sutras, paraphrased as "when organisms are bound by a shared purpose, love cannot help but follow." So are horse and rider bound to one another—true partnership. It's called binomio in Spanish. An ugly word, with no English equivalent, but a delicate, refined significance: two mammals from separate kingdoms joined by a common aim. Which is why it's also easy to fall in love with horses. What I call the Dirty Dancing Syndrome: if you're gonna learn the dance, chances are you, too, will fall in love with Johnny. Or Baby, for that matter. Or both.

After vaulting—learning how to do tricks in order to feel comfortable on the horses—we began learning dressage, the foundation for good ridership. The equivalent of scales for a musician or barre class for a ballet dancer. Dressage sounds cool now, but when I was a kid, it was mind-numbing. I wanted to jump. Jumping was dynamic, high tension. You had to think and act fast. Dressage is the art of cuing, where a shorthand is created between horse and rider. The beauty lies in the subtlety and ease, the sense of togetherness that is established. The goal—breathing together. The outward outcome, a perfectly aligned flow.

English riding is the sport of royalty, after all, which is why Mom took to it, throwing her helmet in the ring as well and deciding to ride with us. Dressage celebrated elegance, beauty, and grace as much as she did. It aligned with her dignified, respectful outlook on life. A perspective that had been passed down from her dad, Papo.

Though Papo probably wouldn't have described himself as either a yogi or a Buddhist, he was studied in both (rare for a Colombian in those days), with the temperament of a Zen master. He was insatiably curious and razor sharp, with a commitment to fairness that garnered recognition amongst his peers. When Mom was little, he had moved their family of six to Bogotá from the small town of el Líbano in the coffee region to become head of gynecology at the new Clínica de Marly. One of the best to this day. When oral contraceptives exploded onto the market in the early '60s, revolutionizing women's lives, Papo wasted no time in advocating for Colombians' right to access birth control, going very much against the grain of his Catholic ethos. And high among other things was his passion for the right to die a dignified death, so he started a foundation for this purpose. Both ideas and practices, requiring a strong backbone and a large dose of wisdom, were beyond progressive for their time—radical even. Shit, they're even radical for ours.

A true seeker, Papo understood the benefits of learning from diverse pools of people and traveled the world, collaborating on the most effective ways in which to share our humanity with one another. His trips, all carefully delineated on a large world map that hung behind his desk, were traced in straight, colorful lines. He'd been everywhere, it seemed.

If asked, he'd tell me stories, sometimes pulling out old carousels of slides, taking my imagination along for the ride with him on his adventures. When I was tasked to write a paper on India in high school, he gave me a private tour—a carousel ride of temples, marketplaces, and deities, not unlike my own pictures when I finally visited. I got my travel bug from him. When I started to explore the world for myself, he always came with me in my heart. Especially when I trekked the Himalayas in Bhutan—a place he never got to visit and one he would've loved—a few months after his passing. When I was as close to the heavens as one can get, it was him I thought of. And when Mom slid her boot into the stirrup to mount, it was his respectful ease that animated her.

Turning eight, I was finally old enough to start show jumping. By then, we were training with the head coach, a lumbering, dusty ex-military man with a handlebar mustache—Major Cardenas. I was a natural jumper. As it turned out, I felt deeply at home in holding the dual tension of the present—the jump I was currently flying over—and that of the future—the jump coming up in my sightline. Our team of thirty included a large cohort of fearless scalawag boys in their late teens and twenties, whom I idolized. As the youngest kid, all I wanted was to impress them.

The Major, stern and methodical when it came to our training, surprisingly filled our downtime at the stables with chaotic, unorthodox pranks. He understood the value of engaging our attention while our country exploded into deeper despair. As people we knew were kidnapped, or killed by thirteen-year-old sicarios in motorcycle shootings. As bombs exploded in our schools, shopping malls, planes, apartment buildings, and newspaper presses, and random acts of violence terrorized the populace. And even though we couldn't understand it all as kids, we could feel it. So the adults were grateful for the safe haven of the stables to keep us out of harm's way and to keep themselves sane in a world that was crashing and crumbling around us.

One of the Major's pranks was the infamous birthday dunk. On your birthday, the older kids would chase you around the stables until you were caught and unceremoniously dumped into the ice-cold, algae-filled drinking trough, leather boots and all. Now that I was officially old enough to start competing, I had secretly decided this was also the year I'd finally get dunked, wedging a towel into my already heavy backpack in preparation. When Mom picked it up to toss it into the boot of the car, surprised by its heft, she asked suspiciously, "Are you carrying bricks in here?" I flashed her the same smile I'd inherited from Dad, making her reluctantly shake her head, letting it go. But as soon as we arrived at the stables and I jumped out of the car guns blazing, racing as fast as my legs would take me, screaming at the top of my lungs like a lunatic, "Come on! Come ON! Dunk ME! DUNK ME!!!" she realized what I'd been scheming.

She found me lying on a pile of fresh sawdust, filthy tear tracks staining my cheeks. No one had chased me. Not one. The older boys, annoyingly protective of my tiny self, had ignored my frantic screaming. Scooping me up with a towel, swatting the sawdust from my hair, she hugged me into her chest until I was done bawling my eyes out.

I earned my stripes a different way.

Merlin, a fast and furious Thoroughbred who lived at the stables, was feared by all. He was light brown with a white diamond on his forehead. When approached, his nostrils flared, eyes bulging from their sockets, and he bared his teeth threateningly. No one rode him. Not even the kids I looked up to. They were crazy but he was wild, prone to taking off like a firebolt, ditching many a rider in a gully or leaving them dangling by a stirrup while dragging them, head in the dirt, all over the stables. He didn't trust people. His owner, an older lady who reeked of vodka, was terrified of him and had all but abandoned him at the stables to die.

Major Cardenas—a savvy matchmaker—had been eyeing me for a while. One day he saddled Merlin and brought him to the arena. Grabbing me under the arms, he swung me onto the saddle before Mom even had a chance to say no. Everyone freezes, including Merlin. He just stands there giving me the side eye, the whites of his eyes pronounced. My insides quiet. Out in the stables, I can hear the squeak of the wheelbarrow stopping as the stable hand scoops concentrate into the feeder—*tssshhh*. Horses flutter with excitement as they knee the stable doors.

Time thickens into molasses.

So Hum

His breath, alive between my legs.

So Hum

I deepen mine to meet his.

My legs don't even extend past the saddle flaps, I'm so small. But he knows I'm here. We wait. I do what comes easy—nothing. Maybe it's just a few seconds or maybe it's an hour, as the distance between us begins to dissolve and we melt into the deep connected space.

And finally, there it is: his permission.

Without hesitation, the Major commands, "Camila, bring him around to the jumps at a light canter. Nice and easy."

We become unbeatable.

Merlin taught me more than how to ride. He taught me his language: that of the breath. Showing me everything that mattered. A distilled and absolute lesson in the arts of listening, truthfulness, and meeting. The Ancients brought the soundtrack of the breath to my ears, but he gifted me its meaning and hidden power. By teaching me how to use it, how to dance. Loving him was synonymous with loving myself. Because he was the first creature to truly see me. He bestowed upon me the surety and steadiness I would need to get through the next thirty-two years. Showing me how to *be* breathed.

The Cavaliers

Ernesto and Marina owned an apartment in Miami where we spent childhood summers. The condo was in a perfectly Floridian compound of cookie-cutter vacation homes that dotted the banks of a pond smelling of duck poop and algae.

Late '80s Miami life was sunny and spacious. People, relaxed and easygoing with their homes left unlocked and apartments smelling of Sara Lee pound cake. Folks looked at you with shiny, attentive eyes and went about their business dressed in unapologetically bright colors. Spanish was spoken in a slurred, lyrical fashion, as if soaked in Cuban rum. Everything clean, safe, and organized— the American Way.

In this almost artificial world, far from the edges of the Bogotá we were growing up in, Susie and I watched *The Price Is Right* weekdays at noon as the sun blared outside. Dolled up in Abuelita's taupe-and-lime paisley apron and mitts, Susie paraded around the living room gesturing at common household items with her right hand, smiling an eerily plastered smile—pretending to be one of Bob Barker's models—while I stared at her, wondering what was so great about mops.

Back in the summer of 1987, Dad was in California studying water treatments for the family flower business. Which grew mostly roses. (Nope, no cocaine.) When I mention this, people always say, "Wow, your dad must've been a great guy..." gazing off into the distance, lost in their own imagination. Envisioning him a bumbling yet disarming Hugh Grant type, manning a quaint flower shop in Costa Rica or Mexico—the only reference most Americans have of Latin America. A bodega with giant windows streaming sunlight, where he artfully designed meaningful bouquets for people to gain their jilted lovers' affections back.

This was far from the case. If anything, Dad leaned hard into his chemical engineering background. He was seriously practical and a bit of a mad genius. A product of his era, he didn't believe in "organic" anything, unapologetically applying pesticides to his flowers and happy to genetically modify them himself to help the business thrive. He could retain numbers in his head better than anyone I knew and later in life funneled his love for chemistry into baking exquisite breads.

The family business gained recognition for its pink hydrangeas, which no other Colombian flower growers had been able to produce. The "how" remains a well-kept family secret to this day. And even though we are no longer in the flower business, it hasn't stopped flower growers from trying to get Tío Gus to give up the gold. The secret was *Dad*.

He kept things low-key in engineering boots, khakis, polo shirts, and cashmere sweaters. A jackknife always handy in one pocket and a wad of loose change, receipts, and credit cards jangling around in the other. At night he dumped the messy contents onto his desk, much to Mom's chagrin—neat as she was.

The farm didn't have a storefront. We were in wholesale exports. Which also meant that during the '80s and '90s around 80 percent of our boxes of flowers were destroyed on their way into the US by DEA agents searching for cocaine, making for some very rough tidings for the business during those years, though that never stopped Dad from bringing a wholesale box of roses home every week. That's twenty-two dozen long-stemmed roses. You read that right. Which were then distributed amongst grandparents, aunts, uncles, cousins, close family friends, and neighbors. But Mom got first dibs. She'd trim the stems at a sharp angle with gardening shears, pull the leaves off the bottom, and arrange them in colorful vases around the house. Dad wouldn't help, per se...but he also wouldn't hold back his opinions as to what should go where, pointing a bossy finger at a surface and demanding a drop of bleach be diluted in their water (for fuller blooms and longer life span).

Dad was a people person, gregarious and abundant. He loved to cook, eat, and hang out. He could hold a conversation with anyone. In his company, everyone was taken care of regardless of state, status, or life situation. He just loved people. Always preparing way more food than anyone could eat in one sitting, making our house the favorite hangout among our friends.

So, yes, I grew up surrounded by beautiful flowers, amidst the intoxicating, delicate scent of roses. Which in retrospect, is extraordinarily romantic...had the guy not been such a pragmatist.

While Dad studied in California, Mom was left to fend for us in Miami. Intimidated by the expansive distances between things, she navigated the roads with utmost care and the help of a dark blue ledger with handwritten notes in pristine penmanship. Notes based on landmarks, not street signs, jotted down by her perfectly manicured hands (hands that modeled for Alka-Seltzer commercials for a period of time). Which meant that year after year, as billboards and shops turned over, we ended up lost in the circuitous Miami infra-structures, praying for a way out. Many tears were shed along the way. Getting lost often meant getting back onto the turnpike, though, where Susie and I fought over who got to toss the quarters into the toll basket, just for the cheap thrill of watching them clank down the drain, through to the other side. Where were they going?

In the States, people hid within the protective armor of their cars. Isolating themselves and also safeguarding their anonymity.

Ahhhhh...anonymity...

The Bogotá I grew up in was as disorganized and cacophonous a place as it was an intimate, familiar one. In Latin America, we build on top of one another like an overcrowded mouth. Thriving in proximity. Which also offers endless fodder for gossip. The sound of telenovelas leaks through open windows; doormen stand out-side their buildings smoking like chimneys; street sellers sing-yell up and down streets, peddling avocados and replacement seals for blenders; recyclers dig through trash after hours, piling their find-ings onto makeshift buggies they then pull down busy thoroughfares at a glacial pace. Horses were outlawed some years ago because they were famished, looking like it was their last rodeo, though sadly, the people who have taken over for them don't look much better. Back then, homeless women held eerily sleeping babies in their arms at traffic lights hoping to tug at your heartstrings for cash. It was an unruly, hard place, with traffic messily bottlenecked, the lines on the pavement mere suggestions. And amidst all of that, the city, on a grid, was easy to navigate with the towering Andes Mountains offer-ing an imposing, lush visual landmark.

Bogotá was in me. In my DNA. It was impossible not to feel it and know it when bumping into someone familiar on the street.

Everyone knew my parents, grandparents, aunts and uncles; knew who was sick, or dying, or who had gotten married. I had a long, deep shared family history with the people in our circles. Which in the end made it impossible for me to stay. I needed space to become who I was to be. We loved hard and congregated hard even within the dangers that existed outside (and sometimes inside) our very walls, and almost *because* of them. It was our way of staving off death. We armored ourselves in life, trust, and community because those were the only weapons we knew, the only ones we had. And they did offer some protection. If not physical, then assuredly mental. Knowing where people came from and being able to place them within the social coordinates of the city helped preserve our safety net as well as perpetuate its inequities.

And because Pablo Escobar wasn't the only disastrous thing that had happened to Colombia—having survived dictators and guerrilla wars—it was not surprising that its society had turned to and been heavily influenced by the *Manual de Carreño*, an etiquette guide first printed in 1853. The manual imitated French and Italian etiquette pamphlets of its kind, suggesting how people ought to behave in public, at home, in school, and at work.

To add unnecessary neuroticism to already crippling societal pressures, Lela—Mom's mom—had clearly mastered said manual. Where some of us had fallen asleep, Lela had digested its teachings ravenously, melding what was on the page with real life. Highly invested in others' opinions, she used the neighbors, the Cavaliers, as an excuse for maintaining extreme composure in all matters and at all times. According to her, the Cavaliers had been watching them all these years. Judging their every move. She constantly peeked out the window, stealthily pulling the drapes up ever so slightly, the delicate orange hue of the streetlamp revealing only one side of her face, making it unclear who was spying on whom. When Mom's family moved a few blocks over, Lela perpetuated this fiction, declaring that these people, the Cavaliers, had also moved right next door. Which they hadn't. She kept insisting that they were watching...always watching. And every move thereafter came with a supposed similar chess move and policing from "esta gente"—the infamous Cavaliers.

Mom, true to her upbringing, tried passing down this code, this etiquette, to Susie and me. And many years later, to my nephew, Santi. Her style, though, somewhat different. A lover of games, mischief, and all things medieval, and knowing her audience well, she called it the School for Pages. Between short-sheeting our beds and preparing us for dinners with the Queen (never specifying which queen, exactly) by teaching us which fork was used when, she made her point. I was a proud member since 1981, having fancied myself after Wart in Disney's *The Sword in the Stone.*

Though we Latins are reserved when it comes to strangers, every aspect of our lives lies open to our immediate family for scrutiny. There is no such thing as privacy, or making a decision alone, or even *being* alone. Everything is a group decision in one way or another. Anonymity, not something we grasped easily. It was a precious gift we knew not of. The anonymity Miami afforded us gave us a welcome rest from our inbred Catholic guilt and meant we could let our guard down if just for a moment. As a family. Something none of us quite knew how to do.

I could sense there were things about me—my makeup—that were unusual, that lived outside the structures of this world. I could sense somehow that in the wrong hands they could be dangerous. Things the Cavaliers ought never be privy to. Things that, if voiced or acted on, would bring shame on our family (the most brutal rung on the social ladder). Revealing things...though I did not know *what* they revealed. And had no clue why. For now, none of that mattered. They remained unspoken truths trapped in the void of stillness behind the mirror. But even a void has shape when examined more closely. As a kid, I folded these truths neatly into my then flat chest like a treasure. Maybe to avoid a misstep. Or, maybe something deeper in me knew to protect them with my Life. Knew that there, folded up against my heart, lay the roadmap to my own unraveling. For me to guard until it was Time.

In Miami, with us all out of context, these illicit behaviors showed up like little bumps in the vinyl instead of scratches. They only added an element of surprise to things, a little grit to the track. They didn't ruin the whole song. Here, we were much more willing to play along the fringes of ourselves and dance with our own destiny. When I wandered to the "wrong" side of the department store and came back holding a muscle T-shirt, Mom simply laughed, surprised but happy to buy it for me. Here it didn't matter if my hair was short. Or if I insisted on pulling the top of my swimsuit down to my hips like a Lost Boy. Or even if I was mistaken for one. Here it didn't matter if Mom laughed too loud. In this alternate universe, we had no one to answer to but ourselves. In this alternate universe, having each other's backs took precedence. We were essential to our family's ecosystem and were loved hard and whole. Lela's rules and the wretched Cavaliers be damned!

Those awkward little hiccups in the Timeline were my favorite. They hold some of the most cherished memories I have of Mom: her sun-kissed face and shoulders, mango dripping all over her hands, giggling almost with glee at my unknowing indiscretions, an infectious look of utter delight in misbehaving, a complicity lighting up her face as she examined me with wonder. How loved it made me feel. The wonder. How beautiful to see it strike. Here we were wild and reckless. Here we were everything we needed. Here we were free. I was loved fully and completely as me. For a window of time that would evaporate when back in Bogotá. I guess that's part of what there is to love about travel: the release from the structures we feel bound by, even if they are self-imposed. That opportunity for reinvention, the chance at discovering things about ourselves always there yet not always present, irresistible.

———

At the pond one day, a man played with a remote-control speedboat. Fascinated, I stared as it skimmed the water's surface, taken by its beauty—sleek, black, and aerodynamic. There was something inherently cheeky in this elegant imitation of the real thing. The engine, rudder, propeller, it all astonished me.

The man handed me the remote. I took it timidly. I'd never played with an adult toy before. The metallic scent of warm batteries flooded me with pleasure as I took it for a small loop around the water. When I went to return it, the man smiled at me. "You should keep it." I didn't understand. "It's yours," he said again, handing it back to me.

Remote in one hand and boat tucked under the other arm, I ran back to the apartment. But my excitement was quickly extinguished by Mom's interrogation. She was not keen on me receiving gifts from strangers. What did the man want with me?

Off we went to find his house. Answering the door, he said, "I want him to have it." A jolt of euphoria zapped my nerve endings, making my cheeks red hot so suddenly that I almost blacked out. My heartbeat, loud between my ears. No one had ever called me a *him* before. On purpose. Mom didn't attempt to correct him, but her whole body tensed. As if our game had been found out. With a dry "thank you," we left. Walking back in the oppressive heat, a small crack formed on the pavement between us. A crack that would grow into a chasm through the years, before we could figure out a way to build a bridge over it. My spirit, receding underwater. Leaving only the sound of my breath for company.

Mom stopped to open the door of our apartment, too worried to see the widening fissure, thinking only of the Cavaliers with a sharp pang of guilt. What she didn't notice was the guilt hitting after the thought, not before.

———

That's when I felt it. The dissonance. Between space and shape. Before, I had been limitless. Mostly space. I knew myself: the space inside myself, the same as the space outside myself. Plainly and simply. Empty—no words or thoughts around it. Not sad empty or lonely empty. Full empty. Assured knowing of myself, empty.

I was boy.

Whatever the girl/boy markers of the world were, they weren't yet exclusive enough to single me out, to tell me that I didn't belong, that I was anything other than what I was. Enough. Whole. I wasn't gauging my being-ness from the outside but rather from the inside. There was no worry. Only ease. It didn't matter what people called me, because I looked and felt boy. Of course, I didn't have anything to compare it to. I was *being* into form. At that age, we are as close to ourselves as we are to one another as ever. There's hardly any distinction. I didn't know then what boys could look like. I didn't care. I didn't have a brother. There was my dad. But he was just that—*my dad.* I guess I didn't think about it, not knowing then that one day sooner than later I would be found lacking, an evolutionary threshold called puberty turning a relatively small and ultimately insignificant bit into the *everything* the world would obsess over and define me by. Puberty, giving me other unwanted bits I would grow to hide.

I remember Susie deciding she was a fashion photographer. Making me model dresses in makeup and sunglasses. She was assembling an album of her work and had me pose in different places around the house. My lips puckered in Mom's red lipstick, shades pulled down the ridge of my nose as I walked around in Mom's heels like I'd seen in magazines and on TV. Delighted in getting to play a girl. For that was exactly what I was doing. A player loving his role. In play was freedom. I was free to be me. Boundless within the walls of my form. With no understanding yet of what those clothes would come to mean. The way they would bind me. Painfully. Sometimes literally. A bind I wouldn't know how to get out of. Perhaps the clearest reason I turned to acting in my college years.

My awareness was beginning to shift.

———

Dear God,

Let me wake up a boy...

Let me wake up a boy...

Let me wake up a boy...

I asked every night. Every night I asked.

I thought...*if I behave, it will happen. One day.*

But what does it mean to behave?

I was already such a good kid.

The Ancients knew:

I was taught to ask...

when I should've been taught to listen.

Let me wake up a boy?

Their answer came, buried within the crashing of the tides:

So Hum.
I am that.

———

It was that same summer that Tío Gus came to stay with us. His thumbs had no fingernails (which was gross and awesome), and his hands were always covered in dark oil streaks from the machines he masterminded for sorting roses.

In his free time, he spent hours building model airplanes from scratch. Putting together the body and engine from elegant blueprints that were permanently laid out on his worktable. I wanted him to teach me the code, how to understand the blueprints. They were like a safe with a glass door, only penetrable if you understood the language. He sanded the wood by hand until it was perfectly smooth to the touch and gave off the fresh, sweet smell of sawdust. Painted in vivid colors, they became stunning works of art.

I dreamt of a day he'd invite me to help him in his workshop. But Gus, meticulous, with a fiery temper, did not factor kids into the world of his hobby. The closest I ever got, along with everyone else, was walking across the narrow dam over the gully onto the neighbor's field to watch his planes fly. They were glorious when airborne.

For the visit, Dad enlisted his youngest brother, Matt (the world's most socially awkward person), who was also in Miami at the time, to buy tickets to a show. At the back of Sweat Records, past endless '80s vinyls and cassettes, was the ticket booth to all the upcoming shows. Skimming the list, Matt's eye landed on Dag Nasty and the 7 Seconds, which to him sounded just like Phil Collins or Juice Newton. He bought five tickets.

When we pulled into the parking lot, empty plastic bags floated aimlessly in the breeze. The place, deserted. The only suggestion of life was the graffitied trailer around back with loud voices erupting out of it.

We waited in the dim theater, the floor still sticky from the night before. It was a blistering evening and the show was due to start soon. Mom, in high-waisted khaki shorts and pink tank top, inspected the tickets wondering if we had the wrong date. A red headband holding her auburn hair in place. Gus, in his customary flannel (even in the heat), checked his watch impatiently. A gesture I emulated only to find with disappointment that my watch—a digital Spider-Man Casio—blinked timelessly 00:00 in punishing dark zeros. *Oh no!* I tapped it several times with my index finger before giving up. It was dead. *Oh well.* I disappeared it into the pocket of my knickers discreetly. I wasn't about to get in trouble again. It was the third watch that had shorted to my touch the same day I'd received it.

Later, I'd sneak into the bathroom and take it apart, looking inside Time herself trying to decipher what made her tick, and more importantly what she was trying to tell me. But for now, it would remain forgotten in my pocket. Again, Time pointing me to my own Timeline. Like Garuda, the half man, half eagle in Indian epic tales who, always the messenger, points people in the right direction saying, "This way, fool!"

Suddenly and without warning, the opening band, Youth of Today, materialized onstage. The lead singer, head shaved and covered in tattoos, leapt through the air like a cheetah, landing at the edge of the stage in a crouch, yelling raw, unintelligible shrieks into the mic at eardrum-ripping volume:

"Please don't expect too much from me
I may not turn out how you want me to be
I'm sorry if I let you down
but I must decide where my future's bound
why don't you just slacken up
off my back your expectations are too much
off my back instead of just letting me be
you've got your goals set for me
I wish you could really be
happy with the real me!"

He was the coolest guy I'd ever seen.

The just-moments-ago empty mosh pit ignited instantly into a cesspool of sweaty, spiky-haired punks thrashing into one another like angry sardines. The first ten rows of seats had been removed to invite the slam dancing pandemonium.

It must've looked odd from the stage: three hundred-plus punks sharing a psychotic episode moshing at the front, while five of us, tucked way in the back, witnessed the anarchy. Susie, twelve years old and mortified, huddled against Mom. While Tío Gus grabbed eight-year-old me by my strawberry suspenders as I tried to make a getaway toward the headbanging. Meanwhile, Tío Matt, looking a little green, was figuring out how he'd explain this massive fuckup to my dad.

A flash occurs. An electric storm shorts everything down to a screeching halt. Time grows viscous, slipping into the slow place, overlapping. Past, present, and future become one for the first time. Punks freeze mid headbang. Sweat droplets shimmering like crystals in the air—suspended. Wind flies through my hair and the electricity *crackles*. The Ancients are with me. The only other person here—the lead singer of the band.

Whispers grow loud around me.

Remember who you are. Remember who you are.

They say.

We lock eyes.

And with a lightning of recognition, just as suddenly, the high-pitched feedback from the amps revved Time back to her normal pace. Music cranked back up. The band picked up right where they'd left off as if nothing happened. The mosh pit reignited with a fury as the window between worlds wove itself back together, leaving in its wake a faint something...a burnt residue I could almost taste.

A terrible itch suddenly gnawed at my back. I tried scratching it to no avail. The spot, just slightly out of reach.

Willy

I grew up with the same classmates from kindergarten through twelfth grade, eighty-nine of them to be exact. Our school, modeled after an American prep school, prided itself on academic rigor. The upside being that I got to wear sports coats and ties; the downside, that girls could only wear pants on Fridays. So it was pleated skirts in the cold, dewy mountain air for me most days. It wasn't supposed to be a Catholic school, but in a majorly Catholic country, it might as well have been. Religion was woven into the fabric of everything.

When Mom brought up my First Communion at dinner, she wasn't really asking how I felt about it; she just wanted to talk over the details. Even so, I respectfully declined.

"I won't be taking communion, thank you. I'm Jewish."

Mom's eyes went wide as saucers. Susie dropped her spoon in her arequipe, and Dad let out an honest-to-God cackle, which just as quickly turned into a cough under Mom's haughty glare. My friend Samuel was Jewish, and he didn't have to get communioned. I didn't

46

want to get communioned either. Which was how I knew I was Jewish too.

I wasn't a fan of Catholicism even then. It wasn't just the vacuous cathedrals and that Mass interrupted the little family time we had. Or that priests looked and smelled like the walking dead in their fancy nightshirts and slippers. It wasn't just because of my religion teacher, Mary Magdalen (her actual name), who at 7:30 a.m. pulled out her guitar and made us bang on our notebooks and desks while yelling, "Sing and dance for the Lord! Praise Be! Praise BEEE!!!" No. The real reason was that I wasn't about to wear a white lace dress with a doily on my head. No way. That much I knew. I had a better understanding of the world now, and I'd begun to find my edges. I dug my heels in further, saying a little louder, "Thanks, but I'm Jewish."

"Honey, you can't just *become* Jewish. You're born into it," Mom tried to explain, frustrated. Dad gave her one of those "I'll take it from here" looks, and we finished dinner in silence.

Afterward, he came to my room and sat on my bed. "Bug, it would really mean a lot to your mother if you'd do this for her."

I crossed my arms. He knew he was losing and so did I. I could be insanely stubborn. I'd sat at the table for days one time when told I couldn't get up if I didn't eat.

"What if I get you a new bicycle?" Bribery. Yes. This could work. I'd only ever ridden Susie's gold hand-me-down.

"A blue one?"

"Sure, if that's what you want."

"Deal." I stuck my hand out and we shook on it.

So it was that I was ushered down the aisle of a church by a boy in a blazer, carrying a white lily in an itchy dress with a white veil, along with the distinctly dusty smell of lace. My spirit crushed like a grape turned raisin. When we got home, though, a blue mountain bike awaited. Photos from that day show Dad with his arm around Mom, pretty pleased with himself; Mom with her arm around Susie, looking at me like she's trying to figure me out; Susie smiling clueless; and me, with a gap-toothed grin, holding onto those handlebars for dear life.

———

As a teenager, I was curious, artsy, and self-consciously shy. A deadly combo in a school that prepped kids for the American Ivy League. Kids from some of the wealthiest families in the country went there. Many of them so rich they were picked up at the end of the day by an entourage of armed bodyguards in bulletproof cars. The drinking age back then was such that if you were tall enough to put money on the counter you could drink whatever they gave you. And nightclubs were open till 5:00 a.m.

Adolescence buried many things inside me, as I was suddenly tasked with something more primal: survival. My gifts dulled and I was cut off from my sixth sense completely, confined by the strictures of this world. I couldn't feel them anymore either—the Ancients. Eventually, I even stopped missing them. I forgot they existed altogether. I stopped seeing the wrinkles in the Timeline; reminders to pay attention went unnoticed. Small vestiges still appeared here and there like the persistent ruined watches...though even that seemed like family folklore.

Puberty struck with a fury. I had no real interest in the things everyone else obsessed over: boys, Marlboro Reds, alcohol, sex, and parties. Until recently I'd been friends with boys. Now they were unrecognizable aliens. I hadn't changed—they had. And there was something I couldn't name that made it impossible to hang out anymore. I burrowed deeper into my love of riding.

Then came Silvie.

Silvie—a redhead, freckled like the galaxy—whom I first noticed at an assembly in fourth grade, had been in the class above mine until she was held back and ended up sitting in front of me in ninth-grade philosophy. We'd never spoken.

One day, when I was caught daydreaming, the teacher made me read a paragraph about the dawning of man out loud as punishment. My eyes stumbled over the word "penis" for the very first time. Confused, I asked innocently, though very much aloud, "What is a penis?" The class erupted. A costly mistake for a teenager, turning me into the butt of all jokes forever more, until, of course, boys wanted me to handle theirs and then no one was laughing.

At the end of class Silvie slipped me a note: "Mila = aloof. Penis = what guys have between their legs." I went beet red under my mop of messy tangles and hung my head over the desk until everyone exited the room. She noticed me. Wait. She *noticed* me.

And suddenly...I *existed*.

We started sending notes back and forth. They made us laugh self-consciously until we got so punchy we were kicked out of class. Once in the hall, we laughed so hard we peed a little from the ridiculousness of it all and were embarrassed by the innocence of our own reaction when we confessed just as much to one another. She took a shine to me. Maybe because I blushed when our eyes met, which made her smile. Or maybe because I let her make little sketches of my hands, fingertips swooping upward as they do naturally, which delighted her.

In tenth grade, out of nowhere, I lost my voice. When I opened my mouth, no sound came out. Nothing. This went on for months. Visits to doctors who pointed and jabbed me yielded nothing. Until one of them identified the problem as acid reflux. The valve at the top of my stomach was malformed, letting acid bubble into my esophagus, making my vocal folds so swollen they were rubbing against one another, forming polyps.

All of a sudden, not only could I not speak, but worse, I couldn't sing. Music was my medium. It was born out of me, an inextricable part, always playing on my Walkman. I was transported by it. I'd sung in a '50s rock and roll band in the eighth grade with some of Susie's friends. My whole understanding of the world—math, reading, space, time, when to cross the street—was music. Rhythm, vibration, timbre, dynamics, reverb, sympathetic vibrations, and pacing were my feelers, the way I moved through space. It offered me resonance where there was none. Now, without it, I felt hopeless. Empty, like a cipher. A nothing.

Within those months of silence, at a dinner at Papo and Lela's, ill-suited for conversation with my notepad and pencil, I was released from social obligations and relegated to Lela's bedroom to watch cable TV.

I was riding before and after school every day by now, training all the testy horses for Colombia's sole Olympic rider. Horses he had been hired to ride himself but couldn't be bothered with. So I rode them instead, for free. I had an edge with these kinds of horses, an eerie calm in impossible situations, coupled with an explosive temper that could detonate at the smallest thing. I was Marina's grandkid after all. This made me a good match for them—both our tempers running picante.

My rigorous schedule, along with competing at the highest levels, left me exhausted, so I welcomed the opportunity to watch TV. We didn't have cable at home. As I flipped through the channels, a made-for-TV movie caught my eye.

The lead—a young woman about my age—starts shuffling through her brother's underwear drawer. I watch, confused and excited. My breath gets jagged as she slides his boxers over her panties and shoves a balled-up wad of socks in her crotch. It feels wrong to watch, but I can't make myself stop. I am transfixed. Something is so dangerous, so familiar here...something I understand somehow, completely.

So Hum

Remember...   *I am that*

Remember

That sound. What is it? It's right on the edge of my mind...

Then it happens. The moment that leaves me agog.

The main character walks out of her room and pauses to look at her name in wooden letters pinned to the bedroom door. Milly. Displeased, she hits the letter M with her index finger, making it spin. The camera zooms in as the letter finally stops. Landing upside down. W—Willy. I am on my feet now, not sure how I got here, jaw dropped, hands on my face, my heart pumping in my ears so loudly I can't hear anything else. In the ocean deep. We stare at it, Willy and I, both simultaneously taking a step back to admire it, mirroring each other in our parallel universes. He, euphoric; me, dumbfounded, still a she.

Willy.

There it is.

What just happened? My internal wires trip. Reminding me of something...a memory.

Flying through the air.
Or was I falling?

Nauseous, I plopped down on the bed. Ashamed. For looking. For seeing. For thinking. For knowing the unknowable, and unknowing everything else. For considering what was being offered. Those truths I had folded against my chest once, now as I looked down, had turned to breasts. A sharp pain folded me over right at the bra line. The weight of my burden winding me, too much to bear.

I can't breathe!

I squeezed my eyes until it receded.
My breath came back...faint.

So Hum

Off balance, I stood up, checking the door to make sure I was alone. Sweating, I straightened my shirt and, with that, shut off the TV, and the door to what could be. I walked out into the living room, a terse smile fixed on my face. As Lela's words buzzed around me, I left my body, not to return for a long time. The volume in the world turned up way too high.

There was no certainty I would recover.

Silvie

Silvie was first to have sex. With boys. Well, girls too...but first, boys. I didn't get how she could walk the next day. "Ask me anything," she said, smudging the butt of her cigarette with the tip of her loafer behind the gear hut in the soccer field.

"Does it hurt?" was the only thing I could think of to write in my notepad.

"Yeah, but it's supposed to feel good, eventually." She looked away, bored.

I cringed.

―――

My voice made a strong recovery. The nodes on my vocal cords were removed, and I changed my diet drastically: no caffeine (making me the only Colombian in history to not drink coffee), no chocolate, no nightshades, no eating after 6:00 p.m., no alcohol, no spices...I was a grandma at fifteen.

I started singing in a band with four boys from my grade. The band, Gardenia, grew popular. It brought notoriety my way that, coupled with Silvie's friendship, gave me free passes to older kids' parties—a much more predatory crowd, one that sniffed vulnerability out like vultures.

Even as girls, our world groomed us to date men. Not boys. Men. We were taught from the beginning that saying *yes* was the only viable option—another vestige from the lovely *Manual de Carreño*. We were to cater to men's every need. Offer them coffee, wash their dishes, cook their meals, serve them, smile when they eyed us hungrily in front of our fathers and commented on how much we'd grown. We were to disregard their expert hands as they crept too low on our backs or grazed our midriff, even as we found a way to slink out of their slimy grasp without making a scene. Good manners were synonymous with pleasing them. As well as cover-ups for the truth of what was there. Men's advances were harmless, as defined by... well, themselves. Our job was to keep the veneer glossy and the lie afloat. Making us, in an even crueler twist of fate, accomplices.

My first boyfriend was twenty-one. I was fourteen. He was a photographer friend of Susie's from college who frequented her apartment. She'd moved up to the third floor of our building, and we'd always shared friends easily. He made out with me at a party at Silvie's and called it *dating*. We dated for three weeks before he finally lured me into his darkroom to show me his photos and then forced himself on me. I froze. Lost my voice again. No sound came to my rescue, while his elderly grandmother watched soap operas in the next room. When it was over, I pulled my pants up, smoothed my hair out, and walked through the living room, smiling pleasantly as I'd been taught. Not sure if what had happened was his fault or mine, or even if there was anything wrong with it at all. For all I knew, that's how things went down. I thanked the old lady for the kindness of having me over. She barely acknowledged me, much more interested in her novela. As he leaned in to kiss me goodbye, my lips swerved out of the way, leaving him with my rude cheek instead.

"That's what happens," Silvie shrugged, pointing to my part in it as she shut the door to our conversation. We all knew the cardinal rule: you could never just leave guys wanting. Soon thereafter, he started dating her. Maybe that was his endgame all along, I'm not sure. Though I was deeply relieved she took him off my hands, my heart broke just the same. She thought I was jealous. And I did feel anger that, I realized many years after the fact, was sadness. Sadness she thought so little of herself as to put herself in that situation. But what did I expect? She, like me, was following the lessons we'd been handed our whole lives. What would it be like to have been given a *no* along with that *yes* or instead of it?

I met Tomás on a family trip to a tiny little island off the coast of Colombia called Providencia. He owned a dilapidated bar on a faraway white sugary beach that looked onto a Caribbean ocean with seven shades of teal. He was charming, easygoing, and mighty fine. Dad was man-crushing on him hard. But Tomás had set his sights on me. He flirted with me openly, asking in front of Dad, "Do you want me to show you around the island?"

Tomás's offer, so inconspicuously laid out in broad daylight, blinded Dad. "That would be great! Honey, you should go!" I'm certain he couldn't tell that Tomás was at least twice my age, since island life ages one slower than the city. When I tried to back out gracefully, Dad said, "¿Qué pasa? He's just trying to do something nice for us. Go!"

Tomás showed up after dinner and lifted me onto the back of his dirt bike. I was in the baggiest shorts and T-shirt I had, feeling exposed already. It was a moonless night, with the Milky Way spreading through the sky like brownie mix. The ground was pitch dark. He hopped on, securing my arms around his waist, saying, "Agárrate." Dad yelled from the door, "¡Me la cuidas!" Tomás smiled broadly and, with a nod and a wink, took off along the edge of the surf as fast as the bike could go, its only headlight busted. The sheen of the water and foam of the waves glowed in the gray of night like lines on a road. We took a hard left up a steep hillside on a jagged trail riddled with stumps and crabs crunching under the tires and came out onto the circular road—the only one on the island. He knew the potholes by heart and drove like a fucking maniac. Terrified, I flattened myself up against him, making myself as compact as possible. Finally, we arrived at the local bar. Not a single tourist in sight. None wanted. As I waited for Tomás to get us drinks, someone pushed me and I tumbled hard onto the dance floor. I was just dusting myself off when he returned, handing me a beer.

I don't remember anything after that. The next morning I woke up not sure of where I was. Susie snored soundly in the bed next to mine, always the excellent sleeper. Throwing on my bikini (the only swimsuit option for Latin girls), I snuck out for the last day of my scuba diving class, feeling queasy the entire time.

Recently, when pressed by a friend, "So what happened?" I realized—that night has no memory attached to it.

———

"Look at me," Silvie demanded, tilting my chin up, holding the lipstick to my face. The condensation of her breath tickled my upper lip. She was a bit of a maven in all things *woman* by now. I had no idea where she had learned it all. She had started modeling and teaching runway classes out of nowhere, even though she was short. What she lacked in height, she made up for in stilettos and a sleek, leopard-like gait.

"I don't think I need it," I complained weakly.

"I know you don't. But you do! Now shut the fuck up and widen your lips like this. Aaaaaahhh." She demonstrated, impatiently widening her mouth into a weird carnival smile that made me laugh. "Hey, I'm not kidding. Do it." So I did. "Aaaaaaahhh." This was the band's first big show, and she wasn't about to let me go out there looking like I'd crawled out of a bird's nest. "OK! Smack your lips together!" She pulled away, eyes narrowing. With one last pass at my hair, fixing a stray, she turned me to face the mirror. "Check you out." Her face, right next to mine, so close I could smell her sandy skin. My cheeks flushed, hands clammy with sweat. The pit in my stomach now knotted into a fist. I wasn't wired for this.

My reflection stared back at me. Wow. I had a nice Chrissie Hynde thing going. My extra-large sleeveless INXS T-shirt hiding my now oversized breasts successfully in its blackness. Without it, my breasts would've preceded me out into the world. An overwhelming development I was not OK with. Navigating them meant learning to navigate the world of men. A choice between two paths: visibility—wearing them like a Viking shield and anticipating their impact; using them purposefully, claiming them before anyone else dared to. *Or* narrowing in on myself—rounding my shoulders over them to let them melt into me, walking the line of invisibility, enjoying the deep darkness of denial and holding on to my innocence for just a moment longer. I chose the latter. This baggy T-shirt softened their definition, the beginning of my extended play with androgyny. A "fuck you" to the boys.

Which backfired. Androgyny wasn't part of gender play in my Latin America. It wasn't really part of anything. I was introducing a whole new visual. Boys didn't know what to do with it. They found it thrilling: the irreverence, the in-betweenness of it, the way it made them doubt themselves just a little. I was unfamiliar, an exotic creature they wanted to have.

The bright red she chose did make my lips pop. The waxy texture giving me cotton mouth. I reached over the sink for some water, and before I knew it I was pushing back tears.

"You're nervous." Her darkly lined auburn eyes analyzed me in the mirror. A different kind of intimacy in them. Lying, though not knowing what about, I shook my head. "They're going to love you," she added, hugging me sideways. "Go knock 'em dead!" I nodded and slipped a round pair of purple sunglasses on. She kissed me a little too close to the mouth.

I might have imagined that part.

In the blackness, my cowboy boots hit the hollow platform clanking with each step as I make my way out onto the stage. The band waits suspended, holding their breath, all eyes on me. I feel the audience for the first time. My audience. I am sixteen.

CLICK! The spotlight beams. Stardust floating against gravity. The silence thick.

Alone.
Under water.

So Hum

Slow and sultry, my voice pierces the dark—

"¡Yo te quiero y deseo tu veneno!
Lo prohibido está en mis manos,
ven pruébalo..."

"I love you and I desire your poison!
All that is forbidden, lies in my hands
Come taste it..."

I eke out time.

Playing with it in my hands,
Manipulate it.

The bass pulls in under me, irresistibly smooth—

"Tú me echas de menos,
mi risa salvaje y mi recuerdo,
criatura de ojos negros
lo sublime te espera."

"You miss me,
My wild laughter and the memory of me
Creature with darkest eyes
The sublime awaits you."

I weave music like a spell...bewitching.

The rest of the band kicks in, locking into the groove.

> "¡Ven, déjame seducirte,
> y llevarte lejos!"

> "Come, let me seduce you,
> And take you far away!"

> *My voice, a conduit—*

> I had them.

Traditionally, the junior class hosted the senior prom, the first formal I'd ever been to. We raised enough money throwing fashion shows and other bizarre events I wasn't a part of to rent a swanky hall at the Gun Club. Buchanan's whisky, the sanctioned drink for the night, accompanied by a twelve-piece salsa band. Girls had dresses made, including me: a sleek low-riding little black dress with a tutu skirt that fanned out at the bottom. Silvie chose my heels, the tallest we could find. The night of the party, she gave me brief but complete instructions while caking makeup onto my face: "Walk toes first and cross your legs as you walk. And Miu, try not to fall on your face!" Then she put hot rollers in my hair and curled my eyelashes while I made faces. When she finally released me, not even my sister recognized me.

"You look beautiful," Checho exclaimed in his gentle way. I adored him. He was twenty-four and a rock climber friend of mine, always respectful and sweet, nothing like the other vulture boys and men around me.

"Thanks." I blushed. And for a moment, I felt it too. Though I'd harbored a secret crush on him the last few years, I wasn't willing to risk losing the sweetness of our friendship.

The party raged until four in the morning. People danced on tables and sang with the band, hammered. Discarded heels delineated the dance floor. When the place finally kicked us out, I thanked Checho and sent him home. He had done enough by coming with me and acting as my shield. I piled into a friend's car with all the other kids and went downtown for a typical Colombian breakfast—soup with chunks of meat in it. The perfect hangover antidote. Afterward, we went to La Paloma, an overlook in La Calera, the highest part of the city, with views to the entire north side of Bogotá. This was the way it was done. Every year.

La Paloma—the dove—a sign of the forever hopeful yet failed peace process between the government and the guerrilla, was painted on a giant rock with a string of blue lace in her mouth. A tiendita next to it sold cerveza and aguardiente. Drunk, we climbed the rock, heels in hand. I admired my shredded hose as I sat there at the top of the world. Mom's shawl doing little to keep me warm in the cold, dewy morning. A boy whose face I have since forgotten made drunk but stubborn passes at me, his shirt untucked and unbuttoned with his fly open and ready to go. I fended him off until he passed out, past the point of caring and knowing he wouldn't remember any of this when he woke up. There, amidst his snores and the sloppy sounds of my peers making out around me, the city's stunning beauty took my breath away in its waking hours.

———

Piles of school supplies were left strewn on my bedroom floor. Finishing our work had taken us deep into the night until, exhausted, we fell asleep spooning in my twin bed, fully clothed. It was a school night, senior year, and Silvie and I had an important project due. She wasn't all that interested in academics, so I'd ended up doing most of it as usual. I didn't care.

In the morning, Mom came to wake us and, seeing us lying there, together, innocently wrapped around each other, she panicked. Pinching the back of my arm hard, she hauled me out of bed half asleep and into her room, where she slammed the door shut behind us.

"What have you *done*?" she raged in my face.

"What do you mean?" I could count the times I'd seen her angry, really angry with me, on one hand. Over the years she'd *threatened* to throw her chancla, her slipper, at me a couple of times, and on one occasion it had even gone whizzing past my head, hitting the closet door behind me. But I had never seen her like this—this was altogether different.

"The two of you, *sleeping* in the same bed!?"

"Nothing happened!" I defended myself, not even fully understanding what she was accusing me of.

"Don't you EVER bring shame on your family like this again! Do you *hear* me?" she growled.

I nodded, a terrified promise. I wouldn't. *Ever* again. I swore.

At that moment, Dad walked in from his shower, clueless, the smell of Head & Shoulders trailing behind him. "¿Qué pasó? What did I miss?"

And though I meant it, it turned out I couldn't keep that promise. I didn't want to bring shame on my family, I really didn't. But I would. Again. And again and again. Until I used up all the shame that existed inside of me and no more shame was left. Until I understood the shame I had been carrying for so long was not mine nor my family's but inherited cultural shame.

Not only was Mom's biggest fear true, there was an even bigger threat neither of us could imagine that would feel even more insurmountable. There was more to me than any of us could have fathomed. It was also inevitable. Because despite my earnest, well-meant promise, nothing could change what was mine to live.

———

I paused at the door, took a deep breath to muster up my courage, and pushed. With the jingle of a bell, the door slid open.

"Buenos días. ¿En qué le puedo ayudar?" The man at the counter was writing something down.

"I need a tuxedo." He looked up at the sound of my voice.

"Is it for you, señorita? Is it for a play?"

"No. Yes. Sure. Whatever." I held my ground, even if a little thrown.

"What's your size?"

"I've no idea." I looked down.

His expert eye sized me up.

"Try this and this." He handed me a shirt and pants. Latin men are small, fortunately. It wasn't hard to find a good fit. The finishing touch came with a shiny pair of black patent leather shoes.

I paid and walked briskly back to the house, hugging the garment bag. It would be another hour before Mom was home. Letting myself in, I hung it behind my riding cassock in the closet. No one would look in there. It wasn't that Mom would try to stop me. She didn't believe in meddling in my business like that. But I didn't want her disapproval souring my resolve. My decision had been made. Even if it was social suicide.

It was the end of high school, and people were throwing lavish black tie parties for graduation. I was bound for Salt Lake City in a couple of months to study acting at a conservatory program at the University of Utah. Before heading to what sounded like the middle of nowhere, I wanted to feel what it was like to wear a tux—the elegance of it, the lines of my shoulders made broader and boxier by the edges of the coat itself.

I changed at a girlfriend's, along with a bunch of other girls. When I walked shyly out of the bathroom—bowtie clipped into place with my hair slicked back into a baby butch ponytail—everyone froze mid-mascara. My friend's mom put the curler down without missing a beat and straightened my bow tie, brushing a mota, a piece of lint, off my jacket. With a wink and a smile she added, "¡Eso, Guapo! You look devastatingly handsome."

Her words and smile annihilated me. The tenderness in them. They made me feel deserving. They stung too. Or maybe it was the tears in my eyes. She made me feel seen—naked in my eveningwear. I didn't quite know what to do with that.

I felt like some otherworldly, magical creature only she could see. As if I had a glorious pair of wings emanating from my back. I imagined a gust of wind ruffling their long golden feathers. Absentmindedly, she brushed a mota off of them too. Wait, what? It tickled.

She was the first in a line of sentries, or emissaries: people, sometimes close, sometimes perfect strangers, who led me along my path. Moments like this began to define me more than all the moments of erasure. A delicate string of beads, a mala, of a different kind of truth being strung along the way. It wasn't that the other life was any less true. There was just a different one here too, in the shadow. The fact that she saw it brought it to life. I could feel the significance, the portent in her look, without having any clue as to what it meant. The oddest feeling in the world is having a perfect stranger see something in you that you don't yet know about yourself.

Tío Ricardo

D ad and I flew over Salt Lake City. Part of me hadn't wanted to look it up in the *Encyclopedia Britannica* to protect myself from knowing how far I was going and all I was leaving behind. The only way to leave was to gaze forward. As the flight made way, I could feel myself shedding the skin of my past life. But when I peeked out the window, my heart sank. The Salt Flats were visible along with the Great Salt Lake. There was nothing there but salt and a weird-looking castle. This was a bad idea. Dad glanced over my shoulder. He must've felt it too, because he patted my leg nervously and said, "You're gonna be all right, kiddo."

I wasn't sure if he was convincing me or himself.

Once in Salt Lake, we were clearly foreigners. They hadn't seen the likes of us before and were mostly confused when we said we were from Colombia. The university? No. That's spelled with a *u*. Ohio? No, that's Columbus. British Columbia? Sure. Whatever. That's the one. But people were decent all the same, which I was perfectly happy with. With the prospect of leaving his baby behind, Dad was more suspicious. But he helped me move into my dorm room with the large duffel bag that held all my possessions, including a thick folder of beloved CDs. We bought bedding and towels and other necessities, and he was so stressed that he ended up going with me to all the orientation events. The only dad there. I didn't mind even if it made me "that kid." The reality of having to say goodbye to him was starting to set in.

Entering PAB, the Performing Arts Building, however, felt like a confirmation that I had landed exactly where I needed to be. It wasn't much compared to other buildings of its kind, I later learned from other students, but to me, the expansive rehearsal studios lined with ballet bars and windows beaming in light were a dream come true. Colombia was such a poor country and had been in a national state of emergency for so long that we didn't have much left to invest in the arts. I was so blown away by the size and scope of the dedicated space that I flopped belly down on the hardwood floor, hardly believing my eyes. Dad stood there a little confused and embarrassed.

As a final parting gift he gave me yet another bicycle. I hadn't ridden since the blue one from my First Communion. I took it out for a spin, and on the way down the mountain from Red Butte Garden, I mistakenly pressed only the front brake, flipping myself over the handlebars and falling right on top of my helmetless head. I'm pretty sure I had a bad concussion, but I didn't say anything because I didn't want to spoil Dad's last night with me. He took me out to dinner even though I wasn't feeling very well, but I rallied without complaint. Then he kissed me and hugged me hard, saying, "I love you, Bug. Try not to fall in love with a Mormon." And with a wink and tears in his eyes, he turned to go, emotion raw in his voice. I watched him drive away, doubting every decision that had brought me to this moment and feeling this new loneliness like lead.

When I woke the next morning, the first day of classes, I had a massive headache and my face felt puffy. I ran into someone on the way to the bathroom and her eyes widened as she scurried into her room. When I looked in the mirror, I understood why. I had two seriously black eyes. Regardless, I was not about to miss class and let my family down after the Herculean effort they'd made to get me here. I pulled out a map of campus and fumbled my way down the hill on foot. People were pretty freaked out by my appearance. One classmate later confessed they thought I'd been beaten. Things were off to an amazing start.

———

That summer, the first gay bar opened in Bogotá—Cinema. That summer Silvie was still in Colombia, failing law school. She wanted to go dancing—at Cinema.

"You should dress a little gayer," she said offhandedly, then changed her mind midway. "Actually, never mind."

"What does that mean?" I fired back, a little miffed.

"Nothing." I stared at her unrelenting until she gave in. "It's just that you kind of already look gay."

"I look gay?" I demanded. She nodded tentatively. "I look *GAY???*"

"Ummm, yeah, you do."

"UGH! I don't even know what that *means*!!!" I sputtered, feeling judged. And I didn't. I mean, I knew what it meant in print, but not what it meant in *practice*. I had no opinions on the matter. It was a blind spot.

That summer I got over myself and went dancing at the gay bar where people looked gay, like me. And my looking game must've been strong because that summer, that which was latent in me turned... like a vampire. That summer, I became GAYGAYGAYGAYGAY. Say it with me.

To be fair, I wasn't the only one harboring a little gay in me. That summer, Silvie and I talked in the car until 3:00 a.m. after gay dancing and when I leaned in to kiss her cheek goodbye, like a good Colombian, she kissed me back. And NOT on my cheek. That summer, the minute her lips touched mine, a thick cello string deep in my spine was plucked so hard I melted into ashes from the volcano that erupted inside me. That summer, the pain of raw desire incinerated me, doubling me over, as the gay phoenix in me arose triumphant. That summer Silvie had a boyfriend...and a girlfriend... and that summer I didn't give a shit. That summer I wanted to dangle from her lips like a rock climber. Put my space boots on and connect her freckles to the stars, turning intergalactic and exploring all the meteors in between. That summer I became an astronaut. Finding myself bereft of gravity altogether and relinquishing my weightlessness into space. That summer was the first time I owned my desire. It was also the first time desire owned me. That summer I was wanted. And it awakened a raw savageness inside of me that found us making out behind closed doors and tasting our bodies in childhood spaces. That summer we were found out by a friend who claimed, "You need help!" which we shrugged off, agreeing with her, and by Susie who asked, "What are you two doing in the dark?" To which we replied, "Nothing." Which was true because we weren't *doing* anything; rather, we were being *un*done. That summer I couldn't be bothered to care. Because that summer, I felt alive for the very first time. That summer there were no words, only meaning; words would come later. That summer I realized I'd been madly in love with Silvie since that day back in fourth grade when I'd spotted her from afar at the assembly.

And that summer my in-love was requited by being in-loved back.

At the end of that summer, I left. My heart in Colombia. Returning to school.

———

On my first day of school as a sophomore, conservatory students from each class performed for one another. Todd, an incoming freshman, four years my elder, blew us all away. The faculty did something unprecedented—they bumped him up to my class.

Todd and I became fast friends. He was gay, closeted, and "passed" easily. In the '90s, for an actor, that was thought of as a good thing. We were happy to get any scraps we could. When the world doesn't like what you are, hiding in plain sight is the next best thing. And it meant he could work. Masculine and tall, with thick brown hair, he was the only Mormon in his family—Mormon by choice—and wore garments (chastity underwear). He was hilarious and smart, and I felt immediately at ease with his charming small-town humility encased in humor and dapper good looks.

Todd confided in me, telling me he moved to SLC to be with his "friend" Jake, a dancer at Brigham Young University. The "roommates" shared a two-bedroom apartment in Provo, one of the suburbs. If found out, Jake would be expelled. BYU had a no-tolerance policy where the gays were concerned. Though they sure knew how to make 'em. If there's something Mormons do well, it's make gay babies.

I guess he figured my Colombian-ness was as far as he could get from his church, so I was a safe haven in which to lay his worries. I was warm, accenting my stories with touch for emphasis (offending and exciting his nerve endings equally), the opposite of the physically reserved stock he hailed from.

Not having my own words, I latched onto his. Now that summer was over, my heart was in a tusa, in knots. The reflection of Silvie's face as she peered back at me through the car mirror was seared into my mind, her cheeks flushed with desire. I couldn't stop thinking about the sun on her skin. Her warm hand under the table playing with my leg. The salty scent of her neck.

Todd offered me context and a backdoor ticket to a life I could never have dreamt of. I welcomed his friendship like a thirsty person welcomes water. He knew how to live within the secrets. He could teach me the code. And he needed a vault, someone to store his most precious thoughts. Silent and impenetrable. So the shadow wouldn't swallow him whole. He needed a mirror to reflect back to him that he existed. That his love was worthy. A resonant field. And he picked me, not even sure if I met all the qualifications, purely because I didn't want anything from him. Women always wanted something. He was, after all, Ralph Fiennes kind of fine. Their desire made him feel trapped. I, on the other hand, made him feel known.

On the day we met, we joked we would marry when my visa ran out. On the day we met, we also almost died in a six-car pileup on the freeway—which he avoided with impeccable timing, a left-hand signal, and a quick lane change.

We escaped unscathed and bound for life.

———

By junior year, Jake had cheated on Todd and Silvie had explained to me, not for the first or last time, that she wasn't "like" me. Whatever the fuck that meant.

Hearts broken for the very first time, we did what people do. We became infatuated with people as unattainable as the stars: two straight friends who were in love with one another. In the throes of youth, nobody thought this was a bad idea, or really, thought at all. Instead, we took a road trip to San Francisco together, the four of us.

Todd and I, following the two of them around like lovesick puppies. And though our obsession reached a dead end, California offered me much more than I'd bargained for.

"My cousin, your Tío Ricardo, lives there. Call him," Dad bossed before hanging up. This was news to me. I'd never heard of a *Tío Ricardo*. So I called.

Tío's house sat atop a steep hill in Bernal Heights, conveniently located near one of the country's oldest lesbian dive bars—the Wild Side West. Its once-fuchsia outside had faded into what Papo called burro al trote: donkey trotting, or nondescript brown. A lush bougainvillea framed the entrance.

I rang the bell. After a long wait the door opened to a tiny Yorkie, Beebee, wagging her tail, followed by a giant Santa Claus in overalls with a snowy white beard. Large, crooked nose and twinkling eyes, he immediately pulled me into his bosom, smothering me. I loved him instantly.

"Camila! I'n so happy ju he'ar, daalin! I'n bery fond of ju father," he exclaimed in a gravelly voice. Then, turning to a pint-size replica of himself who waited patiently behind him, "Denny, chee he'ar."

Danny held my hand in both of his. "Welcome, welcome," eyes twinkling at me like the daughter he never had.

Wait. There were gay people in my family? In my family, the word *gay* had never been uttered. In my family, the word *gay* did not exist. But THERE WERE *GAY PEOPLE* IN MY FAMILY. This possibility had never even occurred to me. Had I not come to San Francisco, would I ever have *known*?

As we climbed up the basement steps, Danny and Ricardo told us the story of how they'd come to live here. Thirty years ago, while looking for a house to buy, this one happened on the market. Though it was a huge property (for San Francisco), with an old barn and a large garden, nobody would touch it. There was a hitch: the little old lady who owned it—Pearl—with no family left, wanted to die in it. What others considered an absolute deal breaker was a no-brainer for two gay men living in a world ravaged by AIDS and a hostile lack of acceptance. They bought the house with Pearl in it, making her a fixture in their lives, for they knew the value of chosen family. Everyone was delighted.

With her permission they converted the top floor into an ample apartment for her and took care of her: bought groceries, cooked, cleaned, made sure she was stocked with toilet paper and all the essentials, and spent time with her. Then, seven years later, they held her hand as she died the way she'd wanted—in her own home.

That's how they inherited this heavenly slice of San Francisco—for their kindness. But they didn't see it that way. For them it was never a choice. Pearl had collided with their path and, as such, had become theirs. They knew they were bound to her. The samurai way. An obvious way to be of service. That's who they were.

This house wasn't just a house. It was a gateway, a portal that alchemized love into action. A doorway into another way of being. Another way of living. A world unknown to me and one in which I very much existed. Here, I had resonance. As is. Here, I felt my self, who I was when I walked in, disintegrating on the way up those steps, leaving the dust behind me.

This house wasn't just a house; it was an architectural wonder of structures piled charmingly on top of one another. Tío, a retired architect, had connected the barn to the house. Light poured from floor-to-ceiling windows into all of its unusual nooks and crannies. Everything was lush, exaggerated, and dusty, maybe from the crumbling of all the selves I was leaving behind. Or maybe because this happened to everyone who set foot in here.

In a little solarium off the living room they called the crazy room, miscellanea stuck to the walls. Everything from G.I. Joes, a kite, an abandoned tutu, fake flowers, scarves, bras, a high heel, a Barbie head, and an old Christmas tree permanently celebrating itself in the corner—remnants of parties past, as well as a willful indicator of the joys of this very moment. The art on the walls was theirs too. Underwear stuck to canvases from the late '70s (when they stopped wearing any), sculptures of lion heads and *cocks* (as Tío called his roosters). "The dyke nex' door gabe me dis gwan! Chee's a lawjer and a tof cukie. I luv me a giant cock!" he said, pointing at a large, colorful ceramic one that sat in the middle of the garden. His hearty laugh, crinkling his nose with mischief. My favorite piece, displayed shamelessly on the garden wall, was a mosaic of the two of them in their birthday suits, re-creating Michelangelo's *The Creation of Adam*. Provocative artifacts in this queer queendom.

I had an immediate bond with these two men. They, like me, had lived on the fringes of society. And they, like me, recognized it the minute we met.

This house wasn't just a house. Their long dining table was adorned with an oversized bowl of fake fruit—very Colombian. Things felt playful, pleasurable, lived in, delighted in. Sitting at the table, Tío piled the lunch he'd made on huge plates. Then regaled us with the story of the time Abuelo Ernesto and Tío Matt called out of the blue on a random Sunday: "Mijo, estamos en San Francisco. We'll be there in half an hour." It was Pride weekend and they'd thrown a rager the night before. Not only were there still half-naked men draped on every surface, but the house reeked of alcohol and the fishy smell of the paella Tío had made from scratch. Springing into action, they gathered bottles, kicked friends off the floor, and slid the giant windows open to air the place out. By the time the doorbell rang everything looked more or less civilized. Ricardo's introduction of Danny as his "friend" made Matt squirm, and in the rush, they hadn't noticed the hot-pink feather boa hiding under the couch. Until Abuelo Ernesto sat down, making its tail pop out. "Yu chould hab seen yu abuelito's face!" Ricardo cackled, smacking his thigh repeatedly, crying, he was laughing so hard. Then he concluded, "Yu need to come down for de parade, Chugar Bowl. So yu can see the dykes on bikes coming down Market Street like farts in the wind!"

These were my people.

This gorgeous expression of bohemian life, an irreverent manifesto for a life I could have, stood as a beacon on the Bernal Heights hill. Here, for the first time, I experienced the matrix of the webbing inside my heart as real. Love was powerful in this place, and worth it. Love won against all the odds. It was capable of amazing things. Unbelievable things. Changing lives, even. It was breathtaking. I was coming up for air for the very first time.

Here, alongside love, saudade, a kind of sadness that has no translation from the Portuguese, abounded. The kind of sadness of what could've been, mixed with a splash of what was. Deep, like the wail of a sailor stranded at sea with no way home. Brave, full, complicated lives had been lived and celebrated within these walls. All of them, gone now. Ricardo and Danny, the sole survivors out of all their friends from the AIDS crisis. It broke my heart to think of it. Feel it in the space. And I also found it incredibly uplifting that such joie de vivre stood within the rubble of a society more than willing to let its beautiful gay people die over something as uninspired and pathetic as sameness.

I'd never met gay adults before...or even imagined them. Though by now I was beginning to suspect I might become one myself one day. And I'd never imagined a fully expressed lifelong partnership. I guess part of me thought at some point I'd have to give up the wonder and revert back to the templates I knew. It's not that it ever felt like a phase. It was more that it hadn't felt possible. Like one day I would have to grow up and betray myself completely, let my soul shrivel into a nothing and walk down the road so many others had before me, sucking it up and dying a slow, lackluster death in the land of straightness. But here, life shimmered. Life held magic. Things were possible for the very first time. I was possible.

This house wasn't just a house. It was a home. A place I could become.

———

My junior year at Utah, the film *Boys Don't Cry* was released. It was 1999. I took myself to the theater to see it. I've always loved the dark solitude of an almost empty theater. Having not read the reviews, I knew next to nothing about the film. As a young artist, I preferred the benefit of having my own experience over other's opinions. But I knew enough to know I couldn't miss it. It was a Wednesday afternoon, and only one other person was there.

You know when you see Marlon Brando for the first time in *A Streetcar Named Desire*? And you gasp audibly?! Because there's nothing else you can do? The take that blinds you with the delicate sublimity of sheer beauty? For me, seeing Brandon Teena was like, whoa...a million times that.

What are you? An angel? A god? I've never seen anyone like you before.

Everything STOPS. I'm in the emptiness. The whole emptiness. Underwater, bubbles suspended. The *so hum* of my breath metered by my heart pounding in my chest.

Glued to the fuzzy velvet of the seat, my whole body freezes. My jaw drops with awe so palpable I don't breathe the entire stretch of the film for fear I might miss something. Any clue. The only life left in me by the end—the need to throw up.

My heart drops out from under me, leaving a hollow recognition in its place: the little boy that was. The man that could've been? This body. A recognition so empty and buried in pain so nauseating, it has the surprising effect of expanding me. Making me more capable somehow of looking—of knowing. And still I can't understand *what* exactly I am looking at. Maybe that is the problem. Maybe this isn't meant to be an exact experience.

I've never seen Hilary Swank before, don't know her art or her name. My rational brain confounded, I think—is she *pretending* to be a *boy*? Is he an *actual* boy? Playing a *girl*, playing a *boy*? Is she *supposed to be* a boy or a girl? I can't make sense of it. I am wholly perplexed.

The thought of admitting this now, as I write it all down, makes me cringe. These are the very questions people feel so entitled to ask me about my kind. Questions that numb. Questions I've learned the hard way are the *wrong questions*. Questions about parts and fits. Questions whose answers change nothing and matter little. But I have to forgive myself, and sometimes you, because I, too, was shaped in a world that at every turn erases us, crippled by the fear of our difference. How was I to learn about all of this? Gain just enough know-how to get where I needed to be? Other than by doing it the hard way? There was no one to imitate or emulate, no one to model myself after. I had never seen my kind before. For all I knew up until this point, we didn't exist at all. We were made-up musings, dreams of a world that could be. I had stumbled upon a few magical guides who had gently nudged me forth unknowingly. The recognition, just enough to inch me along that extra skosh.

The other thing that astonishes me now is that the film is *explicit* from the beginning that Brandon is transgender. Even though it was released in 1999, the movie does not shy away from that truth at all. There is no question. They talk about it unapologetically within the first five minutes. Hormones are mentioned as well as therapy. He doesn't adhere to his deadname (birth name). He even tries explaining everything to Lana, who *knows* though she doesn't quite seem to *understand*. She loves him, which slays me in a guttural way, because I, too, have been on the receiving end of that kind of love. A love that looks at me that way: confused but admiring, with fierce protectiveness. And even though it was completely and entirely clear that Brandon was transgender, I, like Lana, *couldn't fucking see it.*

Why?

Because I had no words for it, no images. No context. I understood that Brandon was somehow a boy, but I couldn't comprehend the complexity of it, couldn't get from point A to point B. I was like Pinocchio *the marionette*, watching Pinocchio *the real boy*, wondering how the fuck it happened. How do I get *there*? The Brandon in me simply didn't seem possible. Maybe it's not only that we cannot be what we cannot see. Maybe it goes the other way too:

we cannot see what we cannot be.

Still, in the belly of that dark, empty theater, a small ember of possibility sparked.

A *what if,*

a *could be...*

And then my emotions plummeted from reverence to sheer horror—cover your eyes with your hands kind of horror—witnessing the sickening reality of the violence that took Brandon's life. A violence inflicted on his gender, his sex and every inch of who he was in the world. Meant to diminish, humiliate, and dominate in the most absolute and final way. By the end it was clear that whatever my connection to Brandon was didn't matter, because it could and should never be acknowledged. The Cavaliers, as it turned out, were not the worst of what I had to fear.

It's something. To see yourself for the first time as such a sublime creature meeting such a violent end.

When Todd and I drove across the country to get me to my internship in Minneapolis after graduation, he needed to pee near Humboldt, Nebraska, where Brandon was murdered. I shook my head decidedly. "You're just gonna have to hold it."

Kali

When Durga, Mother of the Universe, rides her lioness into battle with the demon Mahisa, she becomes so enraged that her anger bursts from her forehead in the form of Kali, the fierce Goddess of Endings.

Kali is most often depicted with her scarlet tongue sticking out, white teeth bare, eyes bulging from their sockets. A mala of skulls, those of the demons she's killed, dangles from her neck, signifying the masks we wear to protect our fragile egos. In one of her many flailing arms waves a severed head still dripping blood from its roots, while in another, the sword that freed it from its shoulders. And in yet another arm, she holds a dish collecting the blood from the decapitated head. She stands over her lover, Shiva, God of Destruction, one foot pressing down on his neck, pinning him to the ground.

When adharma, lack of harmony, takes over the universe, Kali has no choice but to devour everything in creation amidst the chaos. She is both the black hole and the very soil under our feet—all creating and all consuming.

Sometimes the only way to start over is to tear the thing out by its roots, give it a total and finite ending.

As I unpacked my Chucks and my guitar into Tío and Danny's hay-loft in preparation for my first day of grad school at the American Conservatory Theater, I thought back to my first visit to this charming old house: the girl evanescing on her way up the steps to find a new form. After stacking my books onto the shelves and hanging the rest of my T-shirts and jeans on the old costume rack I found in the basement, I jumped on the bed. Arms crossed behind my head, I looked up, studying the red and teal painting of the naked woman with oversized feet who hung there, overseeing my new space, feeling the thrill of her feminine verve.

The year before, Silvie had visited me during my apprenticeship at the Children's Theatre Company in Minneapolis. We hadn't been lovers in years but found ourselves rolling around like wildlings on my living room floor. Which came with a mix of unapologetic abandon and shame.

After she left, lonely and tired of living in hiding, and a bit worse for the wear, I called Mom. I had always loved Silvie more than she loved me. That was baked into our dynamic. And now that we were back in the lover space, I was left without a best friend to confide in. So, I tentatively confided in Mom, asking her, "Have you ever felt more for a girlfriend?"

"What do you mean?" she responded.

"I think I'm in love with a girl."

I was met with the dense silence that freezes hell over.

"Mom, are you still there?" I thought she'd hung up on me.

Instead, she changed the subject after a very pregnant pause. "Your sister won't be able to come visit you in January due to her new teaching post. So, it will just be us."

In her mind, that part of the conversation never happened. We never spoke of it again. I was devastated.

But here in San Francisco, the girl whose desire had been invisible was slowly penciling herself back onto the paper with the help of the vibrant California light, this house, and the oil painting of a naked woman safeguarding her adventures. With still a very long way to go, my life felt closer to one worth living.

Looking out into the garden, daydreaming, I spied an alternate version of myself making out with a lovesick brunette on the creaky wooden swing by the gate, nothing to hide. As our tongues danced like dolphins, the overhanging tree threatened playfully to drop a lemon on our heads.

———

I was hard at work rehearsing the role of Jacinta Condor, a Peruvian billionaire with a Ponzi scheme, in Caryl Churchill's impossible play *Serious Money*. It was 2002, my last year in grad school, and I was excited to play an intricately flawed, wealthy Latina, going against the grain of the usual storyline.

The piece, written in Churchill's signature style of prose mixed in with poetry and song, was proving challenging for me. I was struggling to lift the text off the page. My first scene, a soliloquy to the audience at the top of act 2, was kicking my ass. After a painful hour of watching me hack at it in an empty room, Sebastian Manzi, the director, lost his shit, stood on a chair, and started waving his hands desperately in the air like his hair was on fire.

"No, no, NO! For the love of GOD, STOP *ACTING! You* are the *WILD CARD!* THE SHOWSTOPPER! The whole play hinges on

YOU!" He was so close to me and speaking with so much fervor that his spittle hit my face. Not that he noticed.

"You *open* the *second act!*

"The stage is pitch dark. A spot appears on *YOU*—flying first class, champagne in hand. In sunglasses, a fur coat, and a slinky black dress with your big titties popping out.

"You speak to *us*, the audience. Draw us in, in that *caliente* broken accent about how 'harr laif iis iin Peru,' and gwee. chood. bee. RRRREEVETED!

"I want the audience *AROUSED!* I want every man, woman, and dog to get hard for you, wet for you, whatever the fuck they get for you. I want them to want to *be* you *AND* fuck you! Do you understand me? I want you to *grab us by the BALLS! CAN YOU FUCKING DO THAT!?*

"Get your shit together. We're done here!"

He stormed out.

The stage manager discreetly snuck a tissue into my hand as I gathered my things. I'd been resisting the direction the faculty was pushing me in for the last three years—that of the femme fatale, the Latin stereotype, hypersexualized and exotic. But I had hit a breaking point today. I couldn't play the part if I kept yielding to my discomfort.

Rehearsal had been insufferable. It was time to commit. Never mind that I didn't see myself represented in most stories. I could no longer afford to be so sensitive in a society that didn't want me. I was attempting to make a career as an *actress*. Ellen DeGeneres had come out on TV only five years prior to devastating consequences. The network had dropped her flat on her ass. There was no way forward as myself. No future here. Something had to die. That something was me.

I felt it, my essence, go hard at my center. Heavy and dull like a rock.

Determined, I walked the ten blocks over to the costume shop, wiped my tears at the door, and asked for a push-up bra, a rehearsal dress, and high heels. Tomorrow wasn't going to catch me unprepared.

The next morning I put the costume pieces on one by one, feeling like I was dressing for my own funeral, then slathered makeup on my face, which did nothing to conceal how dead I felt inside. Not enough had changed since the days when Silvie applied it for me, but maybe it still could if I let it. I pulled in closer to the mirror, looking into my own cold eyes. Rage blocked everything. I was numb. I couldn't feel my gift anymore. In fact, I hadn't felt it in years. All the small and large ways I shape-shifted and molded myself had become second nature. And if anyone could shape-shift, it was me, for fuck's sake. Shifting was way easier than traveling through dimensions of time and space. I just had to let myself do it. It was time. To grow up. Evolve. Narrow in. Transform. This was *my* year. The year to become. To show gumption. Fuck Sebastian! Fuck the faculty! I was going to shift so completely, the shape would stick *forever* this time and I would *become* the thing itself. Unrecognizable. *Not just for them. But to prove to myself I could.* I would become a REAL GIRL! *Finally.*

Looking in the mirror, though, I knew I was too late. Staring back at me was a full-blown woman. Not a girl at all. The girl had left the building, taking all of her joy with her. In her place stood a cold, hard bitch. I balled up the tissue with my kiss still stamped on it and tossed it in the trash.

Then, sitting on a rickety wood chair, center stage, boobs up to my throat, holding an empty plastic champagne flute under working lights, sunglasses hiding my dead eyes, I FINALLY BECAME.

Sebastian perched on the edge of his seat, unblinking, wide-eyed, mouthed the words under his breath with me as I spoke them. And he was RIVETED.

A couple of months later, I wandered into a yoga studio for the first time.

The last piece we worked on at ACT, the *Ramayana*, was an adaptation of the epic Hindu poem by the same name. The director, Pedro Rivera, could not have been more different from Sebastian. He had a collaborative theater company in New York that turned ancient texts into daring, mystical theater pieces with shadow puppetry intermixed with live action. Latin, warm, tattooed and pierced like a pin cushion, Pedro wore a mala around his wrist and had an inclusive, expansive approach. He was interested in co-creating the piece with us.

Our class connected to the material and to him immediately. The *Ramayana*, the love story of Prince Rama and Princess Sita who get torn asunder, has many fantastical characters. Among them Hanuman (the monkey king) and Ravana (the evil demon/yogi). Like the original *Star Wars*, it is chock full of mythical creatures with yogic superpowers, ending in an epic battle for the soul, ultimately irresistible to a group of twenty-something-year-olds.

Pedro started every rehearsal by lighting incense. A warm-up of sun salutations followed as the lovely smell of sandalwood permeated the room. When we hit a wall in rehearsal, he meditated on the next right action. No chaos, no frenzy. The road was already there; we just had to uncover it together.

The piece, three and a half hours long, was rigorous. We all played a myriad of roles and were either onstage the whole time or backstage working the shadow puppets. In the first scene, I played one of the king's three wives, having to sit on my shins on hard wood for ten minutes listening, along with my other two sister wives, as the narrators wove their story. When it came time to stand, we were supposed to do it in unison, except that my legs would be so asleep and I'd be in so much pain from the prick of pins and needles that I doubted whether my legs would catch me as I took the next step to leave the stage. I needed more vitality if I was to get through this piece.

On the way home after rehearsal one day, I noticed a yoga studio called (very enthusiastically) It's Yoga! Inspired by Pedro, I walked in. It was a dingy, simple, wide-open room that smelled sweet with sweat. And I loved it in there. The teacher, Reshma, spoke softly, asking impossible things of me yet making them seem plausible through her calm demeanor. Though I hadn't ridden horses since leaving Colombia, there was something deeply familiar and comforting about the audible breath in the room. Like the metronomic flutter of a horse's while galloping—*prrrrr, prrrrrr, prrrrrr*. Like the sound of being underwater when scuba diving. I felt supported by it, a surfer on the waves. And it felt just as thrilling as riding in some odd way. There was an intimacy in it. Like I was riding myself. My own thrust, my own momentum, my own wind horse.

It felt so good, I never left. Sure, I eventually left San Francisco and that specific studio, but I never left yoga. Or perhaps it was yoga that never left me. I had no idea then that the *Ramayana* was one of the seminal texts of yoga and couldn't yet appreciate the symmetry in it being the very thing that brought me to the practice.

As most of me narrowed and froze into a lifeless shell, a small ember still burned in my deepest place. Fanned by my breath, I

tended to it over many years almost unsuspectingly, through practice and then the process of becoming a yoga teacher. Eventually
it ignited a blaze so hot and bright, it not only thawed the frost but
melted everything that wasn't real, leaving only what's essential in
its place. It tempered me too, like the steel of a sword in the fire. I
would rise one day, stronger and seated so well within the fulcrum of
my truth that I would no longer be intimidated.

Marlowe

The spring before graduation, while tripping on shrooms, I inadvertently found myself in a three-way with my friend Cassie and her friend Daphne. Amidst the mess of writhing technicolor body parts, with the leaves of the tree outside murmuring the secrets of the universe at me, I was struck by Daphne's kaleidoscopic green eyes.

Wow.

Her energy, bright like the gold California coast, melted my city edges. Our relationship was born from playful, knowing glances passed back and forth between us. And I was grateful to be rescued from the motorcycle-riding meathead I was seeing, obviously in it for the bike, not having realized that I could have my own one day, sans the dude.

Daphne, younger than me, was just about to graduate from her undergrad program in psychology at UC Berkeley. Even though she was a Californian through and through and belonged among the wildflowers, she agreed to move to New York with me.

We were in love.

I landed in the Big Apple first and found us a small one bedroom in Astoria. Daphne arrived right before the movers came with our stuff.

After unpacking the tea kettle and hooking up the internet, I was on to the next thing: looking for a job. I only had one lead. Nannying. My friend Dana was moving back to Texas and wanted me to take over for the family she worked for. I was hesitant. I liked kids; I just didn't want to be responsible for one.

"I'm only asking that you meet with them. They're expecting you at five. Trust me, you'll thank me later."

"Dana...Dana? Don't hang up! Shit! Fuck."

I needed the money, so I went.

I was a half hour late because I ended up in Brooklyn instead of Tribeca. Rookie mistake. I rang the doorbell, skateboard resting against my leg, thinking this was never going to work. The door opened. A woman with hair like a bird's nest, pencils sticking out of a disheveled bun, enveloped me. "Come in, come in. Dana told us so much about you." I tried apologizing for my lateness but she waved my efforts away, handing me a cool glass of water instead. Noticing my skateboard, she broke out into a really beautiful, imperfect smile, offering me cookies as I sat down in their spacious living room. A small person peeked in from around a corner. "Marlowe, come meet Mila," she said.

The six-year-old walked out shyly, dragging their feet, holding a skateboard of their own, *glimmery wings folded onto their back*.

The room spins. My jaw drops. Blood pumps in my ears. Memories of made-for-TV movies lost deep within the recesses of my consciousness flood back. I am completely disarmed being mirrored so clearly and innocently by this little person. *Did I have wings once too?* I stare at them for what feels like a lifetime...stunned. I've never seen *that*, the *thing* we share, living and breathing, in person, in real life, *the overlap—our kind* so candidly expressed. It renders me speechless.

I hadn't really understood that there were more of us out here.

"Can I see your board?" I recovered.

They held it out like a prize, nodding shyly. It had a gnarly skull on it.

"Wow. That's pretty badass."

Their eyes got big.

"Shit. Sorry. Shit!" I glanced over at the mom awkwardly. She laughed.

"That's probably not the best way to say it. I have a potty mouth." Looking back at the kid, who was blushing. "You probably shouldn't say 'ass' or 'shit' until you're my age. I mean your board is wicked cool."

They lit up.

"Can you start tomorrow?" the mom asked.

The answer, obviously, "Yes!" I never stood a chance. Dana knew. I couldn't wait to spend time with that kid.

Daphne

In the two years we'd been in New York, Daphne and I had carved out a rich, sweet life together. The first time either of us had ever lived with a partner, we were basking in the ever-freshness of it all. Like all good lesbians, we adopted a black cat, Hermione, a nod to Daphne's witchy Halloween birthday. Built a bookshelf out of bricks and boards, stocking it with queer classics, poetry, an array of self help books, and my collection of young adult novels, then decorated it with plants. We learned to cook meals that were respectful to both her vegetarianism and my lack thereof. Switched over to soy milk instead of milk milk. Tried minimizing our plastic consumption and trash output, and experimented with all sorts of natural toothpastes and cleaning products. We even got a rosemary bush, decorated it like a Christmas tree, and hung up three stockings for the holidays— the third with a mighty pawprint.

As for living in New York in our mid-twenties, it was mind-blowing and raw. Daphne worked offering services to unhoused people in Manhattan, which meant she knew everyone's names on the street within a certain city radius. Her day started at 3:30 a.m. and the work was grueling, but also fulfilling. Whereas I took a desperation job at Urban Outfitters when Marlowe's family moved back to Israel. When my manager, frustrated with my inability to neatly fold shirts and sweaters, put a box cutter in my hands and pointed me toward the stockroom, I discovered one of my hidden talents. Creating order where most couldn't appreciate it—by unpacking boxes and building furniture. A mindless job, and I'll probably stroke out if I ever hear "Drop It Like It's Hot" again, but I made new friends and it was easy enough that I could focus on trying to land acting work. I was the "girl next door" (as my sleazy agent would say) by morning and a swashbuckling, drill-wielding dyke in the afternoons. It wasn't glamorous and we were barely getting by, but we were doing it together.

Our limited resources also required us to tap into the city's vibrant underbelly. One offering a cornucopia of free adventures. The Met, for example, lets you in by donation (even today) if you're a local, so for the price of a nickel or a dime, we could muse over the Egyptian sarcophagi's tiny feet. There was a stop sign a block away from the MOMA, where patrons stuck their same-day entry stickers so that people like us could reuse them. The Rockettes, Stomp, and the Blue Man Group were always looking for people to fill the house to make them look more popular. There were galleries, parks, and in the summertime, beaches, music, and outdoor movies. All free. Our all-time favorite date was a round-trip ride on the Staten Island Ferry (also free), which came so close to the Statue of Liberty, you could yell from the boat and she'd hear you.

Yet, as nostalgic as those times seem, New York in the early aughts was also a harsh, cold place. By now Daphne had lived with me long enough to understand that the fine print of becoming a lesbian was not all that welcoming when you pulled your magnifying glass up to inspect it. There was rarely a time we were out in the world together when we weren't harassed. Daphne's only gay marker was *my* gayness, bringing with it an unnerving kind of attention. A very beautiful woman, she was already used to—as much as anyone gets "used to"—catcalls and men's unwanted advances, but this was next level. This brand of harassment had an edge of hostility: some of it particularly motivated by a misogynistic, narcissistic fetishizing of us as a couple, some of it blatantly homophobic ranting. And if we won the lottery that day, it was *ding ding ding*—all of the above!

Yay.

Most often, men would invade our space, quite literally penetrating it by inserting themselves between us. Asking suggestively if they could join us, or pointing out loudly and rather obviously to whomever would listen that I did not have a built-in penis. Not realizing that no one (other than themselves) was confused about this fact. Most of the time, I took pity on them, choosing not to emasculate them in front of their friends by explaining how utterly unnecessary penises were, how easy it was to procure one that functioned miraculously—never requiring Viagra, always the right fit and shape—and the countless other benefits of dating someone like me. But on a bad day, I'd retaliate with something along the lines of, "And she's coming home with me! What does that tell you?" Other times, they tried to alienate us from one another by calling me names or shaming me, as if that would lift the veil from her eyes because, as we all know, women find strangers' insults totally hot.

So, Daphne spent a good deal of time defending me, us, herself, from trolls. I mean...we saw it all. The whole gamut of pathetic toxic masculinity played out daily, including the deplorable masturbators. It's something, knowing you're featured in some nasty stranger's spank bank.

These instances weren't pleasant, but considering the times, they were more like surface grievances when it came down to it. They impacted our lives in small ways, and at the end of the day, we could go home together and shut the front door on them knowing tomorrow would bring a new day.

Much tougher were the things about being queer that snuck through the entryway alongside us, the ones we couldn't lock out and sometimes weren't even aware of. The sticky, insidious ones. Walking through the world as a striking beauty had never been easy, but the truth was that Daphne had lost a lot more than the last of her remaining anonymity by mere proximity to me.

———

A couple of months before moving to New York, when we still lived in San Francisco, I'd finally gathered enough courage to make the call. The one to come out to my parents, once and for all. I couldn't foresee what would happen, but I knew enough about myself by then to trust that I could land on my own two feet if needed. So I screwed my courage to the sticking place, dialed up my joy, and hopped on the phone.

Dad picked up. "Hola, viejo, I have great news," I started. "I'm in love! Her name is Daphne." As I continued, the air got denser, the words turning to sludge in my mouth, making them harder to shape. "She's amazing! We're moving to New York together!"

A familiar fist knotted in my belly. I waited. "Honey, if you'd told me this years ago, I would've been stunned, but you know me...I'm a modern man." I could hear the nervousness under his bravado. Then, not quite able to deal, he tossed Mom the phone like a hot potato, trailing off, "Good luck with your mother."

I was relieved to finally tether Mom's memory to his so I could stop sneaking around, and mostly so I'd never have to do *this* again. This was her third notice. The prior two discreetly discarded from the Timeline, perhaps in the hopes that it was just a phase.

I braced myself. "Mom, I'm gay."

She started crying. Whether from fear of the unknown, or because it was a confirmation of something that had been there all along, or because it wasn't a phase after all, or because this part of the road we couldn't walk down together but had to, or because she was afraid for me, or of me—she cried.

Then said, "OK."

There was a long silence. Then she was off the phone. That was it.

Dad had managed to recover well enough in the moment, but he always got away with skirting on the surface of things. Perhaps unfairly, I'd always expected more of Mom. But I couldn't believe that neither of them asked a single thing about Daphne. If someone was taking my kid to the dark side, I'd want to know exactly who they were and what they were about. But if they were curious as to who was making me so happy, it didn't survive the desert of the third space between us. In their minds, my coming out was happening to them, not me. Leaving me with an empty, lonely silence in its place. Perhaps they couldn't wonder because they were afraid, or hurt, or, at the very least, stunned. Maybe, one could even excuse it as correct etiquette, prescribed by the *Manual de Carreño*, which states somewhere, I'm sure, that one ought not meddle in others' business.

But oh...I longed for their meddling. So deeply, I longed for it. That was why I told them in the first place. I wanted them to ask me. Everything. I had five years of sneaking around and partial truths pent up inside of me. I wanted to tell them about her so they could get to know her and love her as much as I did. There was so much there to love. She was the kindest, softest person I'd ever known. She was funny and smart, capable, and damn it, she was gorgeous. And I craved to be known by them, fully. Hoped to be loved within that fullness. It's a long road between tolerance and acceptance. And an even longer one from tolerance to celebration. But, that's what I wanted. I didn't think it was too much to ask. At least I hoped it wasn't. I wasn't doing this *to* them. This wasn't even *about* them. This was about me. And now, the happiest news I'd ever had to share, the thing most worth celebrating—love—was devastating for those closest to me. But it didn't have to be. *Did it?*

Underneath it all, the well of shame gurgled and bubbled, sputtering its tar and threatening to consume me completely. Leaving me to feel, like so many queers before me, that I was not worthy of owning my joy. A core belief, reinforced over and over again by society's moral and social scaffolding, that bled into all sorts of other nooks inside of me: feeling unworthy of pleasure, unworthy of having a thriving career, of making a family, owning property, throwing parties, having a wedding. The cost of this cannot be overstated.

And all of it, just because of who I am. Who I've always been. In my deepest place, I felt undeserving of all the goodness that was happening. And there was so much of it.

But any societal norm, spoken or unspoken, that aims to create a rift between us and those we love should be questioned and contested fiercely, with every fiber of our being, before our own worth and validity are. For it is undigested trash, mindlessly passed down through generations, showing up as the ugliest part of ourselves—and so cleverly masked as love that it fools even us. And it doesn't belong to us. Not here. Not anymore.

At least now the news was out. There was no pretending otherwise.

Silvie called out of the blue one day. I hadn't seen her since before moving to New York. She lived in Boston now and was dating someone new. They were coming into town next weekend for his work.

We decided to meet for a quick bite in Union Square, then skip across the street to the movie theater. It was a bitter cold weekend in winter. She hadn't met Daphne yet, and what's more, she'd never seen me happily coupled.

Daphne was running late, so I met Silvie and her boyfriend at the restaurant. He was on a call, holding what looked like an old-school calculator to his ear. As we sat down I asked Silvie in a hushed tone, "Why is his phone so big?" She said, "It's a Palm Pilot. You've never seen a Palm Pilot before? They're like thousands of dollars."

Daphne arrived in a flurry, apologizing profusely, peeling off her hat and gloves and landing next to me in the booth with a kiss and a smile. Everything seemed hunky-dory, except that Silvie's boyfriend was on the phone the entire time, making it hard to chat. He didn't apologize or seem very interested in hanging out and, even more concerning, he didn't seem all that interested in Silvie.

When we finally stepped out into the cold, Silvie pulled me aside. I thought we were going to hook arms and do a five-minute greatest hits catch-up, but she stopped me instead. "You have to be careful."

Now I was confused. "With what?"

She glared at me like I should know. I shook my head and stuck my hands out, having no idea what she was talking about.

"You can't just go around *kissing* her like that in *public*." She lowered her voice as if she was speaking shameful, dirty words.

I wasn't sure if she was joking. Searching her face for a clue, I realized she decidedly was not. Trying to catch up to what she was saying, my buzz totally shot, I shook my head reflexively. "Daphne is my love."

"Yeah, but with public displays of affection like that, you're just asking for it." The blood drained from my face and hands. The vapor of my jagged breath, the only thing still alive.

"Asking for what, exactly." I spoke slowly. I could feel my eyeballs freeze.

"You know what I'm talking about."

"No, please, say it. Asking for what?" I asked again through cold eyes.

"A hate crime." She held my gaze defiantly with a spark of red-hot fury.

There it was.

I went calm. Scary calm. *Marina* calm. The kind of calm where you can manipulate time, stretch it, and even make fireballs out of your hands. Silvie's turn to go pale, not sure what I would do. To be honest, I wasn't sure either.

That *she*, my first love, my best friend, the one who knew me most in the world—who nonchalantly paraded me around Bogotá that one gay summer, barely able to keep her hands off me—could stand there, in the middle of the sidewalk, and have the gall to pass judgment on *me*. Have the *audacity* to dump her own homophobia, her own self-loathing, and—yeah, I'll fucking say it—her own *jealousy*, while masquerading it all as concern for my safety?

"Daphne is my *love*." I punched every syllable decisively, glaring into her soul. "If you, of all people, don't understand that...if you don't know that I'd rather *die* here, on this very street, kissing her and holding her hand, than live my life hiding in plain sight? Then you don't know me. At all." I held her stare. She wasn't one to cower from a fight. Until she couldn't stand it and looked away.

And suddenly...

I was free.

I sought Daphne, who was standing frozen up ahead, watching us. Draping my arm over her shoulder and pulling her close, I felt surprisingly elated, knowing how completely hers I was. Steering us in the opposite direction, I called out over my shoulder without looking back, "Enjoy New York."

Her man still clueless on his phone.

That same year, Daphne and I were invited to cousin Tati's wedding. Tía Betty, her mom and Dad's sister, had married into old St. Louis money. Highly competitive by nature and a lover of exerting her magnanimity wherever she could, she pioneered gay tolerance in the family by inviting us.

Mom, Cavalier bells a-ringing, was unduly preoccupied with what I would wear, nervous about appearing in high society. The heat was on and I started losing sleep over it, so Daphne and I, like dutiful queers, set to the task of overcompensating. As we walked by the racks at Bloomingdale's, I considered trying on a couple of dresses, but Daphne wasn't having it, and neither was my body— sweating profusely and hyperventilating—making it a full-body *NO*.

After graduating from ACT, I felt huge relief wearing whatever the hell I wanted, finally released from the shackles of the faculty's constant and intrusive eye. Rejecting their advice to always look "fuckable" (their words, not mine), I never wore a skirt to auditions again. This probably came at a cost to my career, but I just couldn't bring myself to do it anymore. If I got cast in a role requiring dresses or skirts, I'd wear the damn things as part of my job, because at least I was getting paid for it. But otherwise, I was done. The whole point of coming out was, frankly, to *be* out and present myself more honestly.

I'd only ever hidden who I was to make others comfortable. Now I was attempting to reverse that dynamic.

So for the wedding, I needed something feminine enough to make my now more visible androgyny palatable—while still feeling like myself. Daphne came back from the racks holding a classic black ladies' pantsuit. Trying it on with a couple of women's dress shirts made me look even gayer. I was almost in tears when we finally found a silk, low-cut champagne-colored top with spaghetti straps that was so classy and understated, even I could appreciate its beauty.

When we popped out of our neighboring dressing rooms to stand in front of the mirror together—me in my suit and top and Daphne in a shimmery green dress that matched her eyes—the results were traffic-stopping. The salesperson who was helping us gasped, "Gorgeous!" with a hand over her heart. And out of nowhere, Daphne burst into tears.

You see, a year earlier, in 2003, the Supreme Court had finally struck down sodomy laws on the federal level, decriminalizing same-sex sex. Until then, you could still get nabbed for being a homo depending on what state you were in. Later that same year, Massachusetts became the first state to legalize same-sex marriage. Then, in February of 2004, San Francisco mayor Gavin Newsom defected from the ranks of government in an intrepid move and started marrying queers on the steps of city hall, ignoring state and federal law. As gays around the US watched the TV coverage, ugly crying. It didn't matter that the licenses he was handing out were practically worthless, only binding in the city of San Francisco—it was the gesture of it all. That one humane break from the status quo made a definitive impact on the road toward marriage equality, though it took another ten years before the Supreme Court ruled to legalize gay marriage on the federal level in 2015.

For Daphne and me, watching the weddings in San Francisco was one of the most euphoric moments in our lives as well as one of the most stressful. Like watching the tip of a giant iceberg splinter and fall into the ocean in slow motion. The tide was turning right before our eyes, which seemed inconceivable, awesome, and completely paralyzing. But it hadn't fully turned yet. We were in the murky middle.

While I fully appreciated the enormity of what was happening, it came with a splash of bitterness. I had never felt a desire to get married, simply because I had never been entitled to it. The idea of marriage only brought to the surface my lack of worthiness in the eyes of the world. I knew that in order to secure all the rights that straight people enjoyed, we had to *call* it marriage. But I, personally, wanted no part of that institution.

For Daphne, as a newer gay, it was different. The moment we stepped out of the women's changing room, all dressed up for someone else's wedding, the desire for a wedding of her own overcame her. As a little girl she'd dreamt of that moment. She'd planned out her ideal celebration in her mind, down to its finest details: the dress, the flowers, the exact area amidst a cathedral of ancient redwoods at Limekiln State Park in Big Sur where it would take place. She even knew how old she'd be.

And it was getting to be that time.

I arrived in St. Louis a day early to squeeze in a little extra time with my best friend and cousin, Tati's brother, Jamie. The next day, Matt, Gus, Dad, and I piled into the minivan they'd rented to pick Daphne up at the airport. When she walked out of the terminal resplendent, olive skin glowing, long brown hair swaying playfully with her stride, green eyes smiling, the three of them turned into bumbling idiots. Making it obvious how much they all looked alike. It was rare to see them all together like that. And like schoolboys, they kept trying to top one another's stories, faces beet red, cracking each other up while avoiding her gaze. I knew what they'd expected. I also knew she wasn't that. The first season of *The L Word* had only just aired, promoting the "groundbreaking" idea that lesbians *could* be attractive—Jennifer Beals–level stunning, even. Until that point, we were all presumed ugly. Women who couldn't find a man. Their reaction was affirming, but also a bit embarrassing. I mean, get a grip, guys! Jamie died laughing when I told him.

Despite how overjoyed I was for Tati, walking into her huge day with Daphne's arm hooked in mine was overwhelming. With all the feelings lingering so close to the surface for both of us, I wanted to yell, "Run, babe, run!" and take off in the opposite direction, my resistance was so visceral. An elegant wonderland had been crafted specifically for the event. With chandeliers sprouting hundreds of my family's white roses. I guess it felt heartbreakingly tragic. The knowing that I would never have this.

The power of the marriage ritual is so old that it carries an undeniable energy with it. One impossible to re-create in any other way. There's the ceremony itself—but even more than that, the tapestry that is woven through subtle space with the little ways in which people thread together and lend their energy to well-wish and uplift the couple. So that even if gay marriage became legal, and we could have a ceremony, it wouldn't necessarily bring all that magic along with it. Because that feeling is not something you can take or fake. It only works if it is freely given. And the ritual *is* beautiful. It *has* magic. If you let it, it will sweep you off your feet in the span of a breath. But deep down, I knew that no matter how I spun it within myself—even if the ceremony was legit and people brought their full selves willingly—being in a relationship in that way, being a bride and existing within the dynamic of ownership, were just not things I wanted.

Making everything even more bittersweet, Daphne and I were a huge hit at the party. Who can resist the warm, joyful, underrepresented lesbian couple. Everyone loves an underdog, after all. And when they're beautiful to boot, well...

As I stood on the sidelines watching Daphne dance with an unusually frisky Tía Betty, I felt so aware of the life I'd dragged her into. I wanted her to have everything she wanted. The life she'd dreamed of. I so wished I'd be able to create that with her someday. My heart brimmed with love.

"I wish I were a lesbian." Tío Gus startled me, puckering his lips in Daphne's direction—such a uniquely Colombian gesture.

And though he had no clue what he was wishing for, I thought to myself, *I bet you do, bud...I bet you do.*

———

Things got gnarly after the wedding. For one thing, in 2005, we gave up our place to move into a bigger apartment with Todd, who'd finally made the move from Salt Lake. He and I had been best friends for eight years by this point, and though he had met Daphne before moving and they'd hit it off fine, something went terribly wrong the moment his suitcase hit the ground. He and Daphne repelled each other like opposite poles on a magnet. I'd mistakenly assumed that their shared love for me would translate easily to one another. But, note to the reader, it doesn't always work that way.

It didn't help that they were both navigating particularly brutal junctures in their lives. After being the golden child at school all those years, Todd crash-landed into the business of acting, where neither his fine looks nor his amazing talent were a guarantee. Things didn't come easy all of a sudden, and it wrecked him. Depressed, he became moody and erratic.

Whereas Daphne, having moved to New York so that I could pursue my acting career, hadn't seen her family in three years and was really missing them. She was also homesick for the Californian sunshine, veggies that weren't half dead, and the ease that so encapsulates the people of the Golden State. Not able to afford going home again for Christmas, she had to stay in frigid New York with Todd, while I went home to Colombia to celebrate Lela's seventy-fifth birthday with extended family, thanks to my parents' generosity.

If the world had seen us as a legitimate couple, perhaps we would have seen more of that in ourselves, making choices that prioritized our relationship differently. But as it stood, Daphne was left worse than alone, with a person she couldn't stand, during Christmas, while I was somewhere on the Colombian coast with no cell reception.

The stresses between us came to a head the night I got back. She burst into tears upon seeing me walk through the door, emotions gushing out of her. A transportation strike had broken out while I was away, shutting down the whole NYC subway system, along with all the buses. In order to keep her job, Daphne had to walk across the Queensboro Bridge in bitterly cold winter squalls with hordes of people. She'd gotten sick after that with no one to care for her, and without proper snow boots or gloves, her feet and hands were still numb.

I'd had no way of knowing about any of this. It was 3:30 a.m., and I'd come from a long day of travel and connections. Daphne came at me with such ferocity that, in my exhaustion, I lost hold of compassion and landed squarely in defensiveness. "You're making me feel like it's my fault."

Which made her furious. "That's not fair; *obviously* it's not your fault. That's not what I'm saying, but yeah! I guess I am angry with you."

"Tell me, then."

"*You* are my family. I'm in New York *because* of you! And you up and left me here, in fucking Antarctica, completely alone, on CHRISTMAS, with HIM!"

Frustrated and guilty, my voice starting to give from stress, I asked, "What should I have done?" Which I regretted immediately. I knew the correct answer even as I heard her say it. I was an idiot.

"I don't need you to *do* anything. I just want you to *listen*. I'm *your family too*! And sometimes, it doesn't *feel* that way. I don't feel like you PRIORITIZE me. And you SHOULD!"

She was crying hysterically now, whipped into such a frenzy that she dragged her suitcase out from under the bed and started pulling out all her drawers and filling it. I watched her, speechless, terrified. Nothing like this had ever happened before.

"*Where* are you *going*?" I asked in a panic, my voice so raspy now it was barely audible.

"To California."

She was leaving me.

We'd been together for almost four years. I knew the one thing that would stop her. The one thing she wanted to hear. Boy, was it hot in here! I couldn't breathe. I tugged at my T-shirt as if that would help. *I can't do this*, I thought, my eyes darting back and forth, desperately trying to come up with an alternative. There was no other way. With everything inside me yelling, *Noooooooooo! Not like this! You're not ready*—I proceeded to do the worst, most damning thing imaginable. Before I could stop myself, I was down on one knee, pleading in a raw, urgent whisper, "MARRY ME!"

She saw me and froze. I'd lost my voice—AGAIN. The layers of emotional subtext running deep.

She looked at me incredulously. "*REALLY?* You mean it?"

And I mouthed, "Yes. Really." But no voice came. Only silence.

In this moment of extreme disintegration, where I'd fallen so far out of alignment with what I knew to be true for myself in order not to hurt her, my spirit was forced to do what the Ancients couldn't. For I could no longer hear them. I hadn't in a long time. They had become a distant, faded memory—a dream. And so my spirit did the only thing it could: stop me from voicing the words.

CRACK.

Daphne had left her body. Landing back into the room suddenly, she looked around, seeing the time on the digital clock blinking **00:00** in bold red. Realizing that my stress had blown out the clock and that she had no idea what time it was, she broke out laughing. I watched, nervous. The laughter only grew. It became so infectious that it made me laugh too, squeaking like a dog toy, making us cackle even harder. That was the best thing about us. We could always laugh, even in the most extreme moments.

"YES!" she shrieked. Jumping up and down, she threw herself into my arms. And just as suddenly, her laughter turned to tears of relief and release. She melted into me, shaking, while I became a leathery, empty pit of myself.

The next day, euphoric, we ran into Tiffany's after work—two renegades, on top of the world. Until we realized we could barely afford the cheapest ring in the store—a thin, silver band with a small stone on it that matched the color of her eyes.

High on the adrenaline, I called home once more. "Mom, Dad, I proposed to Daphne! We're getting married!" For a second I actually thought they'd be happy for me. Their response, dead silence.

Then Dad asked, completely confused, "Can you *do* that?"

Mila

"We're worried about you, Bug," Dad started as soon as we were on the road.

In the year since the proposal, Daphne and I had saved enough for her to come with me to Colombia, my parents helping us with the rest. We were headed to Villa de Leyva, a quaint little town an hour and a half from Bogotá that sits like a time capsule nestled in the Andes Mountains. For Daphne's first time in Colombia, we all tried to make it special. So when my parents asked if I would ride with them, sending Daphne in the other car with Susie, I knew I was in the hot seat.

"We'd love to see you find a way to continue to act while holding on to a job that makes ends meet." Dad chose his words carefully. Mom silent as a tomb in the passenger seat, wringing her hands. She hated these kinds of conversations. They felt like a confrontation to her. "What do you think?"

He wasn't wrong. I'd worked an assortment of minimum-wage jobs, quitting or getting fired whenever I landed an acting gig, only to look for another disposable job when that ended. My goal: to avoid becoming indispensable at any job so that I could still audition. An uncharacteristically tepid, middle of the road approach for one who puts their best into everything.

Dad checked the rearview mirror, taking in my reaction. I sank into myself, feeling completely blindsided and, at age twenty-nine, like a total loser. I was also stunned that he didn't consider Daphne or the soon-to-be enmeshment of our lives in any part of his equation. Not only was I invisible yet again, we were. We didn't exist. As if we weren't an actual thing.

Daphne, five years younger, had her shit together. She already had a stable career with only a bachelor's under her belt. While I had a three-year master's with nothing to show for it, other than a whole lot of heartache. Acting opportunities were few and far between. When they did materialize, it was always just as I'd landed a great survival job. Acting would then pull me out of the city for three months, paying me shit. An endless cycle.

The downside of being an actor is that it's a hard-core addiction. One almost impossible to kick. From the moment I arrived at Utah, all I'd ever wanted to do was act. However, unless I somehow lucked into a big break, nothing significant would change financially. I was caught in the tension between my dreams and reality. Acting, an abusive mistress.

———

Something else was percolating, though—something I couldn't name. The mountain of stressors inherent in being a woman in acting is formidable. The constant pressures to conform to a specific look, a certain weight. The cutthroat audition process that pits you against five times the amount of women as men, for 20 percent of the roles. But the strain I was feeling went beyond that. Brought on by years of reading character breakdowns I couldn't relate to, I started dreading auditions. Not just because of performance anxiety, though that was there too, but because I couldn't coax the roles open. I couldn't find my way in. So, I somewhat unknowingly created a kind of avatar, a representative—*Mila*. An empty shell that looked the part and mouthed the part.

This made me twice removed from the roles I was auditioning for. I was playing at someone who was playing at someone. For a while it made things more manageable because I could compartmentalize the two as separate. But over the long haul, the static of this separation started to take its toll. The energy required for the dual upkeep was unsustainable.

The disconnect had also started to wreak havoc on my mind. It magnified my feeling like an outsider, a pariah. Why couldn't I relate to stories of women my own age? Women just like me? What was *wrong* with me? My dissociation and frustration were mounting in a way I couldn't explain to anyone, let alone my worried parents while trapped in the back seat of their car. So, I stared out the window instead and let the green of the mountains dull my senses, exhausted.

———

Upon our return to Bogotá, Mom came to my room with fresh towels for us and stopped herself before leaving. "Please don't tell your grandparents you are...*together*." We had a lunch planned with our extended family at the farm the next day. "They wouldn't understand and don't need to know about such things."

I stopped short, the towels limp in my hands, mouth agape, not knowing how to respond. I looked at Daphne, the pain wide in her eyes. Naively, I had figured I'd earned some freedom in coming out and being in a committed relationship. I was floored that I was being asked to shove myself (and Daphne) back into the closet, to lie, to hide—after having put it all out there. But it tracked, considering the way in which our togetherness was consistently ignored.

Mom's declaration felt final, though. And it triggered the little kid response in me. I froze. All but disappeared. The only thing left, an old, cobwebby knee-jerk response, straight out of the *Manual de Carreño*. "Sí, señora," I heard myself say, defeated.

When she left the room, Daphne slowly sank onto the bed. No tears, no emotion this time. Only shock. This was the last nail in our coffin and I knew it. I should've defended her, us. But we were on my mom's turf. There was nothing to do or say. With no privacy in the house and no way of having a real conversation about it except in hushed whispers, I pleaded, "I didn't know what to do."

She shook her head numbly and, putting her hand up, said, "I just can't."

With no further discussion, we went on autopilot and did what we were told. The following day, while everyone was having a perfectly lovely and relaxing time with family, we pretended. Pretended we weren't together. We lied to keep the status quo. To keep everything copacetic and make everyone else comfortable. Making ciphers of ourselves. We gritted our teeth over half-truths about our life together. Referred to as my "friend," Daphne wore her grief like a shroud. While I fielded damaging questions about why I never dated and unsolicited advice on how I could find a boyfriend, a petrified smile plastered on my face. Each unknowing microaggression reaping a bigger and bigger part of my soul. And by the end, it was over. There was nothing left. Everything had been taken.

CRAAACK!

That spring, Daphne was accepted into a clinical psychology program at Stanford. She hadn't applied to a single graduate school in New York. We both knew why.

I waited. For her to address it head-on. To stamp on the crack with her foot, smashing us all the way through. But whether from denial or an inability to zoom out far enough to see the obvious, she did not.

One night, I couldn't take it anymore. I stopped her on the way to dinner, grabbing her hand, the one with our ring on it. She turned to face me.

Wow.

She was as beautiful as ever. It had been so long since we'd looked into each other's eyes. Really looked. She was different. She had changed. Her green eyes now, withholding.

"Is it over?" I asked.

She tightened her grip around my hand, cheeks shiny with tears, unable to speak. The split between us now a fault line.

CRAAAAAAAACK!

The piece of concrete I was standing on caved,
taking me with it.

And from the edge of the abyss,
Daphne looked shocked.

But also...relieved.

———

A month later, while I was still in the dark pit of despair, Mom—an interpreter by trade—tried to make amends and lift me out of my depression, asking me to help translate a manual for ExxonMobil. "Honey, you'd be doing me a huge favor." The job paid five thousand dollars—more money than I'd ever seen. Hating my life, I couldn't turn it down.

The manual, delineating the company's protocols on the "clean up" of fauna and flora during oil spills, was a devastating read. A way, I imagine, for the company to look responsible on paper while washing their hands of future ecological disasters they knew they would cause. It was based on the horrific *Exxon Valdez* spill in 1989 that leaked over eleven million gallons of crude oil into the Prince William Sound in Alaska. The largest environmental disaster to date. Already a wreck, I bawled my way through it as I typed.

Ever since moving to New York, I'd been confined to practicing yoga in my living room, as studio classes cost money I didn't have. However, our move had fortuitously coincided with the shift in technology from VHS to DVD. Gaiam, one of the first companies to make yoga videos, sold me a bundle of their now obsolete tapes for thirty bucks. Thrilled, I became the best student Rodney Yee never knew he had—for years.

As I was finishing up the manual, Cyndi Lee's Om Yoga, above the Strand Bookstore in Union Square, announced their upcoming teacher training. I'd been there whenever finances allowed. The studio was spacious and serene, a place one could *be* in a city always ticking. The teachers were articulate and soft-spoken, an antidote to the urban chaos. When I saw their announcement, I knew this was it—the sign I'd been waiting for.

Dad, more and more concerned by my inability to stay afloat, had started dropping not-so-subtle hints, encouraging me to use my degree to teach acting. Claiming it would be a steadier, safer bet. I understood where he was coming from, but it wasn't for me. *Didn't he get that it would be a death sentence for my career?* Or so I thought. I didn't want to be safe, or steady. I was an *artist*. I was young. I wanted to live a little. I wanted high drama. To learn about the human condition. I innocently believed suffering *made* art.

But teaching *yoga*? I could see myself doing *that*. Even if I had no concrete reason to believe I could. It's not like I was especially good at the poses. I mean, who is? Postures are unnatural. Uncomfortable. That's the point. But I knew I liked being in the yoga studio. A lot. And I figured I had a few things going for me. I was an excellent student who loved the material, hungry to learn more. And I had charisma and people skills, which seemed very important for this job. How many yoga teachers do you know without these qualities? *I can fake it 'til I make it*, I thought. *Fuck it! Let's do this!*

I paid for the training outright with the blood money I earned. It felt important to put those funds toward something positive, transmute them, give them new meaning.

Excited to tell my folks, I rang them. "OK, remember our chat? Well, I took in what you said and I have a plan: I'm going to be a *yoga teacher!*"

I was shocked and hurt when Dad yelled into the phone, "¿QUÉ? ¡Esa es la cosa MÁS irresponsable del MUNDO!" like his hair was candela.

Apparently, this was precisely what they had been talking about. Fortunately for me, it was done. The training was paid for and the studio wasn't going to give me my money back. And honestly, I didn't want them to.

Hanging up the phone, I am strangely calm. The wind rustles in the tree outside my Astoria window as the Ancients congregate around me. Their whispers in my hair, tickling my ears. I ache suddenly at how badly I've missed them. Their company always bringing me home to myself. I've been alone with their silence for so long, so many years, I'd almost forgotten them. Feeling so lost. But they're here now. They've been here all along.

Turning toward them, I open my arms. They have their own plans for me, their own timing. Surrounding me, they nudge me forward...gently, setting the hairs on the back of my neck abristle. I have no other choice, and yet, this feels like the first choice I've ever truly made.

I let them take me.

A week after finishing my yoga training, I landed my first teaching audition at a small Pilates studio in Brooklyn. Nervous, I walked past the boxing gym on the second floor, the smell of sweaty leather hanging in the hallway, and rang the bell. A pint-sized woman with a giant personality greeted me with such a warm hug and kiss that she knocked me off my balance. She was *excited* to meet me and assumed I had something to offer.

This experience was already diametrically opposed to that of acting auditions, where the reception was bleak at best. For an actress with no name, vying for one role among hundreds of other women, there was an unspoken understanding that I most likely wouldn't get the part. So it felt like people were always hunched over their desk, not wanting to meet my eye. That seeing my audition was mere formality. I hadn't realized how heavy that knowing was to carry.

The Pilates studio owner, Sugar, a retired Broadway dancer, was one of those simultaneously razzle-dazzle and prickly performers the theater knows so well. Women as magnetic as they are terrifying. We hit it off instantly, and I knew I had the job before even striking a goddamn pose.

You see, I'd been in my fair share of dressing rooms with women like Sugar. Much like my affinity for testy horses, I had a knack with feisty women. My androgyny, my queerness, gave me a leading edge with her. Granting me a free pass from her sharp edges because she already knew she had me beat. At *womaning.* So she fanned her feathers in my face, delighting in the sexual tension induced by my boyish charm, because she didn't consider its thrust penetrating enough to pierce her straightness. So I could roast her in playful, direct ways that women could not, while bowing to her radiant glow in a way men were intimidated to. A match made in heaven for her, and a role I enjoyed playing for the short term. For the sake of harmless flirtation. Because ultimately, I, too, loved the ping of having my masculinity aired. Of feeling the irreverence and power found in the in-between space.

But something else about this felt brand-new. I had not yet been in a situation where the thing that I most feared within myself, the thing that I had struggled to keep hidden all these years, became my secret weapon, professionally. Where my gift *was* the answer. This was groundbreaking. Who I was was desirable here. Not just tolerated, I was accepted. Better yet, I was enthusiastically celebrated. I could fucking *thrive!* I had stumbled onto a side road only I could inhabit. Something I had that others didn't. Allowing it to express itself meant I didn't have to curb or fit myself into the smallest possible box. It meant I could just open the hatches and go. And all the skills I'd learned so painstakingly in acting, those I'd used to stitch into the makeshift armor of my persona, were the very tools that could help me make the life I wanted, if used inversely.

Once out of the building, I stopped midway down the block because my legs were shaking so hard from the rush of euphoria. I'd stumbled onto something real here. And this, I could do. *I could excel at being me.* It had just never occurred to me to try.

Shiva

After being disrespected, the sage Durvasa curses the gods, the Devas, taking away all their power. Desperate, the Devas team up with demons, trying to gain it back. Together they hatch a plan to churn the ocean, attempting to retrieve the nectar of immortality from its depths. But immortality is not to be messed with, not even by the gods themselves. Their efforts unleash a poison so deadly, it threatens to undo the world, along with everything in it—the hala-hala. The Devas, unable to stop the inevitable annihilation, are forced to call Shiva, the Lord of Destruction, the only one powerful enough to help.

Left with no other choice, Shiva swallows the deadly poison, the only way he can think to get rid of it. But he can only swallow it just enough to hold it, imprison it in his throat for all eternity. Knowing that if he swallows it whole, it will destroy even him. The poison, so toxic it quickly turns his throat a dark, deep indigo.

This, some say, is why Shiva's body is often depicted in a light blue hue—from the poison seeping slowly into his skin.

In yogic tradition, the throat center, Vishuddi chakra, is home to our communication: what we are able to convey, to say, and what we aren't, as well as our ability to listen. If blocked, communication between the *material self* and the *timeless self* is hindered, making truth telling, as well as deep listening, nearly impossible. I'd wished for clarity so badly, for things to feel simpler and more straightforward. All the while, unable to listen to what my spirit was telling me.

After a whole life of grappling with my femininity, trying to contain it, hold it somewhere inside of me—from my First Communion, to playing Jacinta Condor, to becoming an almost bride—it had finally bled through, congealed in my viscera. Not fully grasping that gender is a social construct and that humans are capable of far more complexity than society allows, I had gone and done it—turned myself into a real girl.

Now, through the newness of teaching, as amazing as it was to feel the diametric contrast of my own élan, my vitality, my masculinity burgeoning forth, this newfound sense of self destabilized my precarious equilibrium in a way I'd never known. Historically, I'd managed to keep some semblance of balance between the two poles of the gender binary. Now, the more I allowed my masculinity to blossom, the more impossible it became to *perform* femininity.

Even my name became a trap, a sticky, meaningless riddle I couldn't solve. *Mila.* The name I'd used my whole life. The one my parents were so excited about that they found a creative way around its infamy. The name uttered by those who had loved me back. And the one I'd belonged to. Not only had it been co-opted by my actor persona, but worse, it had ceased to feel relevant, ceased to be me.

Society has unleashed the poison. The lie of gender. And it is I who must harbor it in my throat. But I am no god. I do not have an eternity in which to linger suspended. I must either spit the poison out or swallow it whole. If I swallow, I am sure to die. And if I spit—I will destroy my world.

So I fall.

II.

Into the Void

Raghunath

While having brunch at a diner in Hell's Kitchen, my sudden desire to travel to India surprises even me when my friend Dakota mentions he's planning a trip there and I blurt out, "I'm coming with you!" My own voice, a stranger to my ears. The Ancients, in their excitement, making me spill some of the sugar from my teaspoon.

I'm about to turn thirty-two, still single and in desperate need of something to rattle me out of feeling sorry for myself—something life altering. Even if hard. Better if hard. And I have a sneaking suspicion that India will deliver on that front, not even really sure as to why. Maybe because, as Mom puts it when I tell her, "Honey, that's so far away!" even as she and I span the distance between New York and Bogotá. Or maybe because I don't know much about India, even though I should, especially if I'm peddling their philosophies and practices for a living. What I do know, from my years of acting, is that heartbreak, rigor, and exhaustion make an excellent recipe for change. One I desperately need.

That's when I hear his name for the first time: Raghunath. From another teacher, in passing. And it rings so curiously in my ear that it sticks to me like gum.

I venture to take his class for the first time, synchronously, on the same day Dakota confesses he can't make our trip happen after all. He's broke. I understand, obviously. But where does that leave me? I'm still intent on going and know I don't want to go it alone. The desire has taken root, and it feels urgent, necessary—an almost painful physical pull. I *have* to go. Find my way there somehow.

And that's the day. The day I meet Raghunath. Bummed by Dakota's news, I take myself to his class. Movement, the way I work through disappointment as well as everything else in my life. Mat strapped to my back, I find the studio door once more—the first test, since there's no visible signage to either confirm or deny its existence. I'd missed it the first time I'd been here, tucked between a nondescript dollar store and a hole-in-the-wall kiosk selling African CDs. The only suggestion that the studio actually exists is the directory on the side of the building stating its name in small, black, uneven letters.

Once inside, I eye the long litany of steps—four flights of them, to be exact—placed there as if on purpose, as a preliminary weeding device for whiners. They glower back at me defiantly, *Enter at your own risk.*

I start the steep climb with an inhale.

And it is a risk. Entering. The last time I did, the menstrual cup I used for my period exploded as I lowered my legs from headstand. I felt the seal pop as my toes touched down, the burst of warm, viscous liquid soaking through the liner of my shorts. Springing up faster than a ninja, I wove through the packed room in a panic, trying not to kick anyone or stub my toes on the heavy cork blocks (which hurts like hell), praying the blood wasn't visibly running down the insides of my legs yet. Ducking into the sole bathroom, directly adjacent to the studio, I peeled off my shorts and rinsed them in the sink feeling utterly humiliated by my femininity just as the class came into Savasana—corpse pose. Stuck in there without being able to make noise, I lay on the cold cement floor trying to rest. Which brought me just short of a panic attack by the time class let out. A perfect storm of period-related awkwardness. One that mortified me to the core.

My desire to meet Raghunath was so strong that it triumphed over my embarrassment, the only reason to face those stairs of shame again. The studio, at capacity, is lively with chatter. I recognize some faces, hoping they've forgotten mine. It's tough to find a spot, but people around me move without hesitation. A lovely extension of Raghunath's teachings that precedes him into the space. In other yoga rooms, people get downright territorial over their "spot," turning into conquistadores without realizing the yoga *isn't quite working yet.*

A voice booms from the doorway, "Yogis, introduce yourselves to your neighbors." The room erupts into lively greetings. A stocky Italian guy with a shaved head, covered in tattoos, enters, milling carefully around the mats, an instrument that looks like a large wooden box slung on one of his shoulders. Putting it down carefully on the windowsill at the front of the room, he sits next to it amidst the gongs and plants, backlit. With a loud click, he opens the instrument's bellows, pumping air into them. Placing his fingers on the keys, a low drone floods the room.

Soooooooooo
Huuuuuuum

Remember...
A voice calls deep inside me.

"Take a tall seat. Close your eyes. Get your breath going." The room quiets instantly. We all know what we are here to do. Discipline runs strong in this group. Our breath thickens almost into visibility.

So Hum

Re-member...
The word rustles like a memory.

The deep sound, like that of a church organ, permeates the space. Filling all of its nooks and crannies. Seeping into the foundation of everything. Dissolving dense matter into no more than a bunch of tiny vibrating cells that knock into one another like bumper cars, easily molded and reshaped. I am so taken by its awesome sound that it soaks right into my bones. My breath, audible now, gives me a laser-like focus. Like being underwater. Swimming, or rather folding into myself. I drop in. Everything heightens. A huge satisfaction wells within me. That of reconfiguring, restructuring. A kind of coming home I wasn't aware I could access.

"The mantra has a high vibrational tone. It cleanses the energetic body like a loofah, scrubbing it from the inside out. We'll sing together, call and response. It's not the Sanskrit that's being listened to, it's the heart. Try your best." His voice cuts through the room—

Sri Krishna Govinda
Hari Murari
He Nath Narayan
Vasudeva

I stare at him surprised. The image, so dissonant. This hard-looking, scrappy, solid man wailing with a sense of...tenderness...disarms me. The room joins in—all forty-seven of us.

I close my eyes. The meaning of the mantra rings through my entire body. *Let go*, it says, *let go*. It's impossible to find a new order, to reorganize, without letting go. And it must be just what I need to hear, because the fire in my chest is now aflame. The hauntingly beautiful imperfection in the singing humbles me, makes the hard parts of me malleable. And the roaring heat cracks my heart wide open. Rattling my core—

He Govinda
Hari Murari
He Nath Narayan
Vasudeva

Re-member who you are.
There it is again! Calling.

Down I swim, down into my depths, against the tiny bubbles rising. Through Time. And mist. And Space. Diving into the unknown landscapes inside myself. And there, deep within my own infinity I begin to remember something older and wiser than this physical body. Remember the wet that is water. That I am the drop *and* the ocean. Remember my essential tuning, that which makes me—me. I feel the life force carried in my breath. Palpable. And there's something aflutter. On my back. An itch? A tickle. The vibration of the sound, leaving only that which is essential. Clearing all that does not belong, like a flood dragging with it that which has no roots.

Remember...

And so I begin...to remember, like the ember of the fire ignited long ago deep inside me.

I feel my Self, the self who lives parallel to me, the one who could be, but seems not of this world. Fully awake now, for the first time in a very long while, electric. Ignited, my eyes open. My heart throbs, shining molten lava into the space. And somehow I've levitated a whole foot off the ground, head thrown back, chest wide. *Then...I feel them—my wings.*

They flutter open just a hint. Luminescent. The room, vanishing around me as I hover between the worlds. The so hum of the Ancients echoing—suspending me. No longer bound by space. Or Time. I'm in zero gravity, where nothing exists but us. The eternal me and the me bound to this world. My wings spread. Wider than I imagine possible.

Suddenly, Raghu's eyes meet mine. My concentration breaks, and with a loud thud, the floor is back underneath me.

No one notices—the moment gone.

"One spot just opened up for my pilgrimage to India," Raghu yells over the chaos of people putting their props away. "If anyone wants in."

Yes. I want in.

The synchronicity cannot be denied.

Walking up to the front of the room, I introduce myself, shyly. Raghu tilts his head sideways, hugging me. "Have we met?"

The room goes dark.

We have. We've traveled together over many Lifetimes.

"I don't think so...may I come with you to India?"

"India's not for everyone," he says, testing me.

"I imagine that's true."

"Then it might just be for you."

We are on a flight to Delhi that September.

———

Rubbing the jet lag from my eyes, I hand the bright-eyed porter my backpack, palms pressed together at my heart as a thank-you. He piles it onto a rusted old cart held together with a wish. Dawn is breaking, and the air is pregnant with humidity. Delhi, shocking upon first encounter. Its cacophony, an assault on the senses as we walk to the train station not far from the hotel; the cart, whining its disapproval the whole way. Mendicants squat on the roadside, makeshift tents made from plastic garbage bags lining the medians. Children, in hoards—curious and unrelenting—tug at our clothes. Traffic bottlenecks impossibly with an assortment of bicycles, camels, elephants, tuk-tuks, and water ox. The world is alive with all the smells, all the bells and horns, all the colors, and all the feels. Technicolor living and breathing.

Once inside, the train station is a self-contained universe incomprehensible to Westerners. Impossibly crowded with families asleep on every inch of the filthy floor. The atmosphere of abandonment makes it hard to discern whether people are stranded here, waiting for a train, or what they are doing altogether. Gangs of monkeys pound the rusted structures that hold the roof in place, and when I look up, one of them pees on our heads. When the person next to me goes all New Yorker on them, they jeer and scurry away, laughing like hooligans. Raghu throws his hands up in the air exclaiming lightheartedly, "What could go wrong?" People peddle their wares, one of them offering to soup up my backpack with wheels. I shake my head, "chalo, chalo," a phrase I picked up on our walk, meaning—like many things in India—go, go *and* come, come. Mine, an obvious go, go.

People stare as we make our way. Just stare. It feels unnerving. The air of desperation in the thick heat clinging to my skin, like breath itself.

When a train arrives, it slows just enough for people to hop on, never actually stopping. Train cars so crammed people have to elbow their way on.

I struggle to maintain the brisk pace set by our monk guide, a gregarious teddy bear of a fellow named Radha Kundha—with a shaved head and sikha (small ponytail at the back of the head)—who weaves seamlessly through it all, saffron robes swishing as he parts the seas for us effortlessly. The little ponytail, a way for Krishna to pull him back onto the righteous path if he strays, or at least that's what he tells me when I ask. I can't tell if he's joking.

In the commotion, I trip over someone. Turning to apologize, I see it is an old renunciate, a sadhu, who, wearing nothing but a lungi (a cloth wrapped around his genitals), lies in a lotus position on his back—a tipped-over statue—eyes wide, unmoving. I tap our monk's shoulder, who pauses, tilting his head back. "Kundhaji, is that guy dead?"

Glancing back to check, he responds evenly. "Yes. He has left his body," then smiles, bobbing his head, exposing the large gap between his two front teeth, making him even more endearing.

Seeing my jaw drop he quickly adds, "Don't worry. He doesn't mind." And with a good-natured chuckle, he sets off again, weaving through the incremental human tides. I freeze, transfixed on the body. I've never been this close to naked death before. People step over it without so much as a glance, as if it were a suitcase. And someone almost shoves me right onto him again! The push snapping me back into the present moment as I rush to catch up to our group, shaken.

Once in Rishikesh, we try to beat the heat by practicing at 5:30 a.m., while it's still dark. Dawn being the best time for contemplative practices. The stuffy conference room with '70s carpeting smells of mildew and mothballs, the odor so pungent and practice so sweaty that even in the dawning heat, we get into the habit of dipping in the Ganges—or Ganga, as the locals call it—afterward. The hotel, conveniently located on its banks.

It's a sacred experience, that of dunking in those mystical teal waters springing from glaciers high up in the Himalayas. Refreshing and marvelous. As a young mountaineer in Colombia, I'd dreamt of visiting these mountains. And swimming in their waters now, gazing up at their epic peaks, I feel alive, free, and ever so lucky to be here.

Bathing one morning, we spot a group making their way toward us. Raghu bursts out, a little too loud in his enthusiasm, "They're coming to join us!" Only to realize that midway down the line, men are carrying a body wrapped on a makeshift stretcher. Recognizing what is happening immediately, from his days living as a monk, he jumps out of the water, grabbing his shirt, and says, "Let's get out of here. They're coming to burn the body on a pyre."

That afternoon our group goes whitewater rafting. The rapids start high up in the mountains. By now, chanting has become a favorite group pastime. We chant all the way up the side of the mountain in the bus we've named the "Bhakti Bus" (Bhakti, the arm of yoga that focuses on service, and part of what the Vishnavites, the sect we're traveling with, practices), which is heavily adorned on the inside with colorful tassels and has a horn that sounds like it's out of a cartoon.

Chanting naturally elongates your breath, bringing you into balance with your autonomic nervous system and each other, so it is a wonderful way to keep people calm as we shave the sides of the Himalayas on the most dangerous road in the world. The bus has two "drivers." At first, I find it odd. Until it becomes evident why the second guy is there. The road, meant as a two way, is barely wide enough for one vehicle, and there are big chunks of asphalt missing that have tumbled down the slope. The second guy sits opposite the driver, leaning out the window, making sure the wheels are still touching something. Looking down the mountain through the windows, we can see shells of other buses that didn't make it.

We also chant down the river. I know some of the chants by now. Most of them malas, or strings of God's names, others, prayers. As a failed Catholic I'm more than a little leery about singing to God, especially since I don't ascribe to a formal religious view of what that is, but I know the truth of what I felt in the room that first time singing with Raghu. The clarity. And it doesn't feel threatening. It's something altogether different, unfamiliar. I am open to it.

I will later learn that Indian deities are meant to represent aspects of ourselves, like the sides of a prism—that chanting their names taps or wakes up these specific qualities in ourselves in the same way that a mallet striking a gong makes it ring. This makes perfect sense to me. Each varying iteration or name for the same deity invokes a different part of the self. Much like terms of endearment honor different aspects of someone's nature.

The difference in a name, and its vibration, the way in which it evokes distinct reactions, seems as obvious to me as the heat from the sun. This, coupled with the endorphins that accompany the physical act of singing, elicits unadulterated joy in me while chanting. I've sung my whole life and loved it. But I have not experienced joy like this from singing since I was a kid. This feels completely different from what I've been doing all these years and closer to what I was doing while changing into my riding gear in the back of Mom's car. So satisfying. As an actor, there's been a high premium on my being "good" at singing, or doing it "well." This is not that. It is raw, wild, slightly offbeat and often out of tune, and I LOVE it. So does everyone else. The chants are simple on purpose, to make them easy to sing, easy to remember, turning them into what one of my friend's kids calls "earworms"—the kind of infectious tunes that hold your mind hostage so that you cannot stop humming them all day. I learn that this is part of what makes chanting so effective as a way to settle the nervous system and part of its very purpose: to cut through the needless piles of crap in your mind and give it a high vibrational bite to focus on instead. Like the difference between fresh food and packaged food. Giving yourself nourishing sound as opposed to numbing sound. Before I know it, I wake up and go to bed humming the damn mantras, in the same way that I still feel the sway of the ocean when I lie down after surfing.

We belt at the top of our lungs the whole way down the rapids, especially through the scary patches, which is noticeably wearing on our guides, until arriving safely at the banks of the hotel. Then, out of nowhere, the guides start yelling in frenetic Hindi, "Chalo, CHALO!" This one, a definite "Go, GO!" I jump out of the raft, not entirely surprised that they've had it with us, only half aware of the charred smell in the air, and am distracted by little pieces of something black floating in the water. Wondering what it is, I lean down and pull it up to my face to smell it. Soot. Where is it coming from? It is then that I look up to see a dog ripping a long strip of meat hungrily from the torso of the smoldering body, the same one from this morning, and realize what has happened. Hence all the yelling. Burning through a human thorax is no small feat. A fire needs to blaze infernally in order to consume the dense shield of bone and tissue that protects our internal organs. The fire hadn't burned hot enough.

There it is. Everything exposed.

A gasp moves through our group. Leaving people to their shock, I run into the hotel to shower in the same water I'd just been standing in—the only kind available. When my roommate comes in excited to do the same, I can tell she hasn't made the connection yet, and I'm not going to be the one to break it to her.

That's India for you. Everything we take such care to hide and are so precious with in the West, out in plain sight—laid bare, demystified... exposed. Taking the maya—the illusion—out of it. Impermanence at its finest.

Tasha

On an unusually lazy morning in the life of two fledgling yoga teachers, we map each other's bodies through sound. Moans, groans, pulled inhales, and sharp explosive bursts are our sonar. My scrunched eyelids heighten the ecstasy exploding through all my other senses as the sheets, damp and exhausted from our writhing, rip. Neither of us cares. We just melt into each other again, laughing.

I roll onto my back with a culminating sigh, but our hands continue to flutter overhead in their ancient mating ritual of fingers kissing, slipping through each other's negative space, spiraling and coming undone only to collide back into one another's folds. Your crooked smile flashing my way. I know you are self-conscious of it. But right now I couldn't love you more. Maybe it reminds you of your smoking days when your lips curled around a cigarette. Now you only smoke every blue moon to remind yourself you don't have to. I love that smile enough for both of us. Your flushed cheeks slay me. I've never considered having a family until now. I can feel you all, in my future, waiting. I am home.

You've known who I was since the moment you walked by the yoga room. When time slowed just enough that our eyes met, changing everything. I never hid myself from you. I couldn't. You saw right through me from the get-go. We became friends. Not much was at stake then. We could take it or leave it. You were heavily guarded. Not one to let people in. But somehow I did it. I slipped through. It happened by accident when, sitting in the first rays of the spring sunshine in Union Square, you proposed we get a hotel room and be done with it. The attraction was clear. I shook my head and smiled a "not in a million years" kind of no. We were both otherwise part-nered, and I've never been one to cheat.

That small word—no—like an arrowhead, struck the glass pro-tecting your heart, shattering your desire in an instant, but breaking through into something more essential. Its impact, forceful and directed right at the center of your armor. And down through the cracks I swam, unknowingly. Burrowing a part of myself there in your depth.

Many messy months passed. We hurt our people to find our way to one another. Pain—ultimately unavoidable in the realm of love.

I tell you about Willy. About the weird made-for-TV movie—how seeing a girl turn into a boy tugged at the long bass string in my spine, the same one that doubles me over at your touch, tuning me. And in the dusty glow of morning, it seems like somehow I'd imagined the whole thing.

"Tía Vicks always called me Miles," I add sheepishly.

Miles.

I've never said it out loud.

Not a single utterance. All these years it has remained inside me, unstruck, ahata. Only to be drawn out into the light unexpectedly at thirty-five while in bed, besotted.

M   i   l   e   s

I taste every one of its curves. The *mmm* rings me like a bell, tingling; my voice drops into the valley of the open *aaaaiiii*—a mourner's wail; my tongue flicks off the L, daring me to finish, to finally seal it off with the zoomy *zzzz's*—a satisfying bookend that leaves me punch-drunk. It comes out unkempt like a fecund garden—surly and overgrown. I've always loved the irreverence of it—Miles.

We watch it, the name, fly like a hummingbird. Momentarily hovering by the lamp next to our bed. If we are going to catch it, send it back, the time is now. You follow it with your gaze, not a fan of disrupting the natural course of things.

Out it goes into the bright sunlight.

Still looking after it, you ask me, voice raw with emotion, "Would you like me to call you Miles?"

I know how much you love Mila. You've told me so yourself. Love saying it, the sound of it—love this version of me. Mila is your home. Your bravery humbles me. I admire the way you charge forward fearlessly into the complete unknown.

My eyes well, knowing the answer unequivocally and wanting nothing more than to fly out the window after it.

But I stare at you instead, eyes wide with panic, communicating with you silently in my mind. *Can we do that?*

And for a fleeting moment, it feels like we can. We can do anything, you and me, create the world how we want it to be.

But Miles is here now. We have phased him into the room. Willfully and unapologetically, he demands to be known entirely as himself. With him out here I am left with no choice. I must turn to face him. Turning my back on you only so that I might see. What can be.

"Yeah. Say my name," I whisper. Sound shaping into Truth. Breaking the room.

With that I've handed you the truest part of my self—everything that matters. And this time I can feel it.

So I turn to face him, armed in your courage. I look my Self squarely in the eye for the very first time.

I don't know then that I am trading us, you and me, for my own destiny. As a self-identified lesbian, there's nothing here for you. I am male-ish at heart, neither a woman nor a man. Just some sort of boy. When it was a game, we were best friends. Lovers unstoppable. Twin flames. Now that it's in earnest, it is too real. I never imagined how important identity was to you. You were the first to love me like a man, after all. I've never felt attached to mine, being a shape-shifter and moving between so many worlds for so long—always the guest, never the master. What identity did I have the right to? The only identity I'd ever felt at home in was being yours. Where does that leave us?

You feel betrayed by my inability to come back from the game, though you encouraged it. I feel betrayed because you know what you're asking of me. Something we will never find words for. It is you or me. You pit me against myself. Or so I feel. And though I have betrayed that part of me all these years, this time...this time, I cannot reverse the play. My soul digs its heels.

The scaffolding of our love gives way—

I figured when the time came you'd come home...because I am...
still me. But I was naive. Maybe we both were. This isn't the me you
wanted. Either way, it doesn't matter anymore.
I have to fulfill my destiny.
I have to fulfill my destiny.

Tasha?
Babe...

I feel for you through subtle space...
You never answer me again.

My heart, homeless once more,
But my spirit, homeward bound.

You leave, taking my sleep with you.

Miles

I get called in to audition for a birth control commercial for a pharmaceutical company. I'm feeling severely uninspired. I'm still nursing my languishing acting career alongside my bustling yoga teaching, and my universes are pulling farther apart. If I land this gig, though, I'll make enough to float me for the next five months. I might as well go.

I scramble to the westest part of Manhattan, the no-person's land that lies between the West Village and the Meatpacking District, my stilettos and black spaghetti-strap tank top (the only girly things I own), stuffed into my Colombian satchel, my mochila. Upon arrival, I sign in and change in the bathroom. Applying waxy pink lip gloss from an old tube with faded gold lettering and gloppy mascara onto my lashes—the extent of my comprehensive makeover routine—I smack my lips apart and walk out. When I ask for the sides, the woman at the desk informs me that there are none. It's a testimonial. With nothing to prepare, I sit, close my eyes, and settle into the rhythm of my breath, allaying my nerves.

So Hum

"Mila. Mila Borrero?"

"Yeah, that's me...Hi." I stand.

"Headshot and résumé, please." I hand them over, following her into the room.

"Sit on the stool. State your name and height."

"Mila Borrero, five feet six inches."

"Hold your hands up. First the back. Good. Now the palms."

I do as she asks.

"OK. Are you on birth control?"

Wait, what? I panic. I'd been sitting out there waiting for fifteen minutes and it never even occurred to me that a testimonial for a birth control commercial would entail actually *being* on birth control. *What is wrong with me?*

"No."

"Oh, OK. Hmmm. That's OK. Have you used birth control *before?*" she tries helping me.

"No." The veneer is off. I can't even lie. Lifelong exhaustion catches up with me, I'm so far out of my element.

"Oh, OK. Well...this is a commercial for birth control, so we need a testimonial from someone who is on it or has used it before."

"Yeah, um...sorry. I didn't realize I had to use it in order to be eligible for the role."

I'm clearly the only person who has come in here with this problem. Seeing my distress, and realizing that I'm partly right, she strategizes. "It's OK. You're an *actor*, right? So why don't we do this: *pretend* like you have used it..."

"OK." I take a stress breath.

"Are you on birth control?" she asks again from behind the camera.

"Why, yes, yes I am." Heat builds in my cheeks with the lie, my voice an octave higher as I grasp for something to say.

"Why would you recommend it to other women?"

My pupils dilate. I've really never used birth control before. Not once. The men I'd had sex with used condoms, and that was lifetimes ago; I can't even say I would know how to put one of those on a penis. I wrack my brain, but I am so embarrassed by now and feel so singled out that my vision starts to go dark around the edges. The room narrows in on me.

"Mila...can you tell me a little bit about why you'd recommend birth control?"

I stop breathing. I'm sweating profusely. It's so quiet in here that I can hear the blood moving through my veins. I'm light-headed. I might pass out.

"Mila..."

Before I know it, something snaps inside me. I jump off the stool. Not really in control of what I'm doing. And without a word I turn and bolt out the door.

Making it out onto the street, I pull my cell phone out of my pocket, hands shaking, gasping for air as if I'd been holding my breath underwater. I click on my agent's name—let's call her Judy.

Now, I have despised this woman for so long. As long as I've known her. She's like Ursula from *The Little Mermaid* and, I'm certain, the worst agent in all of New York City. I'm not even hyperbolizing. Every time I leave her office, I feel filthy. Like trash. Like I have to take a shower in order to get her ooze off of me. She's brash and mean and has not an ounce of style or grace. And to top it off, for six whole months, she mistook me for a different client, sending me out for Molly Booker's roles...until I got called in for *Crowns* (an all-black cast) and figured it out. Think how furious Molly would be knowing she had missed out on an audition with legendary casting director Bernard Telsey. FUCKING JUDY! I'm walking at a hysterical pace down the sidewalk. "Judy, it's Mila Borrero. Please stop sending me out."

My heel snags in a crag, breaking with a snap. I pull it off my foot, exasperated. "Whaddaya mean?" Judy responds in her gruff Jersey accent.

I realize I'm standing by a trash can and throw the heel in with all my might. "I mean, I'm done. Stop sending me out. I'm done with you! And I'm done with acting! And I'm done with all of it!! Do you hear me? I QUIT!!" I snap the phone shut. It feels so FUCKING GOOD to finally be rid of her. Elated, I laugh like a maniac.

I want to be rid of Mila, the persona too. This stifling costume I've been wearing for years to fit in, to belong, to just earn *the right* to walk into a fucking room, for a shot at a role I don't even want! I'm over it! I rip off the other heel, sending it the way of the first one, and can't stop there. Grabbing the front of my stupid black top, I pull on it, hard. The damn thing won't come undone. Incensed, I peel it over my head yelling, "GET THE FUCK OFF ME!" And before I know it I've thrown it in the trash too. I'm so angry that I grab the sides of the big, nasty, solid trash can and shake it with all my might. It won't budge, it is massive. "AHHHHHHHHHH!!!"

Two passersby stare, jaws agape. I desist, huffing and puffing, embarrassed suddenly. The heat going right out of me, deflating me down the side of the building and onto the ground. Barefoot, in a push-up bra and jeans, holding my head between my legs, hyperventilating, trying desperately to lengthen my exhales so as to not have a full-blown panic attack.

After what feels like an eternity, I manage to calm myself down just enough. *You're OK, you're OK*, I say to myself over and over. I'm certainly not the only person who's ever lost their shit on these streets.

Standing, I realize my mochila is still in the building along with my sneakers and T-shirt. I'd rather die than go back in there. I have my phone, my wallet, and my keys. That's all I need. So, I start walking the two blocks east to Hudson Street, feeling as barefooted, naked, and crazy as I look. A cab pulls over for me—the woman who has lost her damn mind. The cabbie hands me his hoodie without a word as I climb into the back, looking at me through the rearview like, "That bad, huh?" Making me grateful that this city's seen it *all*.

All those years acting, pretending, trying to be somebody else, just to realize the only thing I'd ever wanted, wanted more than anything, was to be myself.

———

Silvie and I didn't speak for four years after the episode in front of the restaurant. When she moved from Boston to New York after Daphne and I finally split, we reconnected. It was not the reckoning I had hoped for. Never good at taking responsibility, she chalked her behavior up to her then douchebag boyfriend. Loyal to a fault, I agreed to bury the hatchet. After that, our sporadic conversations remained on the surface of things.

She calls one day. "I saw you changed your name on Facebook."

"Yeah."

"You didn't tell me!" Her tone, prickly.

"I didn't think it was a big deal." Already weary of this conversation, I just don't feel the need to explain myself.

"Well, it *seems* like a big deal to *me*. It feels like it came out of nowhere," she says, sounding surprised.

This irritates me beyond belief. Can't she see that this is vulnerable and scary for me? Where is her care? Her wild heart? I'm casting a vision of myself into an unknown future. A vision I'm hoping I'll grow into. Manifesting a dream.

Yet again, it feels like she's policing every step of my queerness. Her persistent projection of her fears onto me is numbing.

And it *isn't* completely out of nowhere. I'd started calling myself a boi since before she moved to New York, back when I bought my first packer with Daphne at a sex shop in Soho in the early aughts. I'd never loved labels. Too binding. Dangerous, even. But upon hearing the term—*boi*—I could see it offered a shorthand that no other word could in describing how I felt. Lesbian was exacting, butch wasn't sexy, dyke was a lumber company, and soft butch was someone with a mullet and pink bowling shirt with the name Lacey stitched on the pocket. Boi seemed cool. Not a man, not a boy. Something in between, nonthreatening. A young adult of undetermined finish, which I was. It also seemed wonderfully noncommittal—a perfect in-betweener certificate. A shingle I could hang on the wall of my identity if just for a brief window of Time.

"I have always been this way," I say dully, then add, "Nothing has changed." This, a lie. The chasm between us has widened so far I need binoculars to see her in the distance. While she's afraid I'm killing off the old version of myself and, therefore, the old version of us, I wonder—*is it such a bad thing?* The us that existed was one completely defined by her rules. It seems to me we are in store for a much-needed reincarnation. With our present, living in the past.

And something else has changed. Me. My need. I need backup. Fierce warrior backup. Old-school, no bullshit, no frills, no questions asked, Kali, Angel of Death shit. I need Silvie to go to bloody war for me, murder and pillage if need be. Not task me to clarify, justify, or give her a reason why. I need her to champion me. Say, "Miles. Miles! I LOVE that name! From now on you will be Miles." That's it.

Where she needs to control, I need her to throw me a fucking rager. And just this once, I need it to be *about me*.

———

The heart of Raghu's teachings is distilled in this koan—

> *I am not the body*
> *I am not the mind*
> *I am something divine*

Words that set in motion profound healing for me. Hearing that who I am is perfect, divine even...is *radical*. Diametrically opposed to the worldview I've been handed up until now—that of a lowly sinner. They also feel aligned with the world I'd like to live in. A whole, connected, abundant world. So I glom onto them, the words. They become a kind of mantra, a code. My spiritual compass. My North as I navigate these new, uncharted waters. Revealing a way of life where there's space for everyone's unique gift. Making me, us, you and me, greater than the sum of our parts. I take the words to heart and for a while, they fill my life with a sense of belonging and purpose I have lacked.

> *I am not the body*
> *I am not the mind*
> *I am something divine*

But, as healing goes sometimes: I begin to unravel. For this mantra holds one of the most impossible, confusing riddles of my life. On the one hand, it says I am worthy—*as is*. Divine! On the other:

if I am enough, why do I feel like I need to change something essential about myself? Especially something material?

A deep dissonance gnaws constantly at me now. I've been aware though unaware of its existence for as long as I can remember. Corseting myself too tightly all these years—literally, with the bra that pancakes my breasts painfully against my chest—has restrained the thunder from rising just enough. But the elastic is about to give way. I feel this *something* stalking every inch of negative space inside me, like a caged animal ready to break loose.

Sensing the epic come-apart, I discipline the ancient depths of myself with these teachings, secretly punishing my desire to change. If this body is truly just a rental for this lifetime, then what does my biology matter? Just because someone *has* a Mercedes doesn't mean they *are* the Mercedes. Isn't it about the driver, not the car? Then what does my sex matter? What does what people, or I, think of it, or call it, matter? This is an amazing body, isn't it? It's healthy, works hard for me. I've even come to terms with the way it looks. I've never hated it, even though aspects of it make me uncomfortable. That's just the price of admission on being human, no? Bodies are weird. What more can I possibly want? Maybe I can just ride it out for this lifetime.

And yet, my yogic discipline does little to quell the nagging question, *Wouldn't life be so much better without my breasts?*

Ahhhhhhhhhhhhhhhh!

There it is.

I am not the body
I am not the mind
I am something divine

No. The teachings imply I can learn to exist *as is*. Within my duality. Quell these feelings through practice. Which is how I turn these beloved words into the double-edged razor I use to become a spiritual cutter. Making small, just painful enough incisions in my subtle body every time my spirit digs its heels in, yelling, "YOU'RE GOING THE WRONG WAY!"

I AM NOT THE BODY
I AM NOT THE MIND
I AM SOMETHING DIVINE

AHHHHHHHHHHH!

Until I realize...just how wrong I've been.

———

At the airport in India, before flying back from Mumbai, I bought a sticker of Kali, without knowing why. Though Dad's health has been steady the last few years, soon after my return, he winds up in the ICU for three weeks. He can't breathe. The decline, sudden and steep. Pulmonary fibrosis—his illness—has no cure, and his lung capacity is so low now that he is permanently on oxygen. It is clear that I must carve a new relationship with Death. Mostly so that I can survive his.

I paste the sticker on the cover of my journal and stare at it. Making Kali the gatekeeper to my thoughts, which are now blank pages. Completely silent. I cannot see past the wall in front of me. Fear shrouds everything in darkness. When I look, I only see her—monstrous, aggressive, and so over the top it is almost absurd. So different from all other religious depictions I grew up with—mostly those of Christ bleeding on the cross—which are also dark. But Kali, in comparison, is downright gory and wild. *And does Shiva look like he's enjoying her foot pressing down on his neck?* There's something so BDSM about the whole thing.

My mind wanders aimlessly through all these distractions as I grapple with my feelings around Dad's imminent death. As well as my reaction to the deaths I encountered in India. The effect they had on me was diametrically opposed to that of my Indian siblings. Death doesn't frighten them, and they grew up with these terrifying images of it. This fascinates me. They grieve Death, sure, but their response lacks the heat of panic. Mine is only panic. Maybe seeing the worst of Death depicted daily takes the sting out of it. I definitely feel that as Kali's bulging eyes stare back at me. Her maniacal presence is sort of soothing. Maybe it's the representation thing. Maybe seeing Death allows me to come to terms with it?

My Catholic upbringing raised me to fear every one of Death's aspects, including the material body's part in it, making it seem repugnant. I'm sure growing up with rampant kidnappings, murders, daily bombings, and a newsfeed littered with massacres didn't help. Attacks were random on purpose, specifically to cause terror. No pattern could be detected. A politician assassinated on a commercial flight by the person seated directly behind him. Another flight hijacked with a handful of Americans on it, as well as a friend of ours from riding (only a year older than I was). When released, four and a half years later with Stockholm syndrome and a debilitating autoimmune disease from living with the guerrilla in the jungle, her family was broken and bankrupt. Another friend showed up with a gnarled piece of car bomb—as big as a human torso—that came crashing in through her window when the shopping mall across the street exploded. There was nothing to do but cover our mouths and gasp, "Are you OK?"

"The walls are black and the windows blown, but other than that, no major damage," was her response.

Can you imagine? *No major damage.* That's how it was. How we lived. When my parents were out late, I waited up for them, petrified, running through all the scenarios as to why they'd never return. And I wouldn't even describe myself as a naturally paranoid person. Anytime I left the house, I had to tell them where I was so they knew to search for me in the rubble if something happened.

And horrible things *did* happen. Every day.

In ninth grade, the same year I lost my voice, while Mom was still working in admissions at our school, the phone rang in her office. When she picked up, a voice at the other end said, "There's a bomb in your school. You have half an hour to get everyone out." When I spotted her in the soccer field, I knew immediately this was not a drill.

So, I grew up afraid of Death. Very afraid. Because I needed to be.

Maybe this, the trauma of living in a war zone, coupled with Catholic fastidiousness and the unwillingness to grapple with our own mud, was part of what made Abuelita Marina turn her back on Life so stubbornly without so much as a challenge from anyone. Maybe we were all stunted into a sort of freeze mode around Death and had been for so long, we didn't even know it. Allowing Marina to claim her throne—or bed, as the case was—and rule with relentless power, inflicting the ugly pain she couldn't assuage inside herself on everyone who remained. To then die over ten long years. From boredom.

I'd always felt incapable of wrapping my brain around what compelled her to do such a thing. Not realizing, until now, how much her decision had marred me. It wasn't just the calling it quits and waiting for Death to find her, though the implicit drama in that is worthy of *One Hundred Years of Solitude*. It was more the *way* in which she exacted her power over Dad and Tío Gus through the infinite days turned years, demanding that they, and in turn we, uphold the very Catholic kind of penance of visiting her every single night. A brutal demand openly thwarting our ability to live our own lives, and more specifically, Dad's and Tío Gus's ability to live theirs. Chipping away at the tapestry of their family life one day at a time, strategically. As if to say, if *I* choose Death, *you* will all go down with me. Which is why we sat, night after night in that stuffy bedroom reeking of old, milky body and sheets, staring at her dentures fizzing away in the sepia glass on her nightstand, listening to her gums smacking while she lay there like a lump, judging us, saying, "Ayyyyy...¿Qué más? Ayyyyy...Pft...Pft..." day after day after day.

Until she threatened Mom, that is. That's when Mom put an end to it, finally. It turned out that to add to Marina's abusive, narcissistic tendencies was a long-time addiction to uppers that had gone either unnoticed or unacknowledged. The uppers, originally prescribed for weight loss, had become the thing that kept her from shattering all the gorgeous china she had so expensively brought back from actual China. So when she underwent hip surgery from being bed-ridden and neglected to tell the doctor about the medication, her withdrawal manifested as the psychotic episode that ended it all, where she threatened Mom with her walker like a caged animal. No one knows exactly what was said. But that's how the family found out about the pills. When it happened, teenaged Susie was standing outside the door with Papo, who didn't miss a beat to bring home the pros of a dignified death: "People have an expiration date too, Susie. Entiendes? It's important to honor that." After that, we never went back to visit Marina at night. From then on, Dad had to go it alone.

Now, looking back, I'm struck by how much Marina's decision to not get out of bed over those ten years rocked me to my core. But what was even worse was the unspoken agreement between adults to act as if this were normal. As if Death somehow was so frightening that the mere mention of it gave a person, in this case Marina, carte blanche to behave as badly as she wanted for as long as she did.

In the West, we reduce Death to the moment the heart stops. Diving headfirst into Eastern philosophy, I learned that a comprehensive body of knowledge already exists on this subject. They honor Death as a process: the delicate and gradual uncoupling of consciousness from the material body. *How* the tethers are disentangled is the very source of their study. Their outlook, much steadier and oddly sweet in its acceptance of the realities that come with Death. I say *oddly* because there's no trace of tenderness or warmth in regards to someone's passing in Catholicism. It's all fire and brimstone. The Eastern view is gentler, allows for space in the dealings of the spirit as well as the earthiness of the body, which feels grounded, wholehearted. Monks have spent thousands of years studying each one of its stages.

Learning something as simple and profound as the fact that hearing is the first sense to enter the body as well as the last to leave it is deeply comforting to me. It is the reason we instinctively talk to babies and play music for them before they are fully baked and why we talk to people as they are exiting. Tantric Buddhism has the *Bardo Thödol* (*The Tibetan Book of the Dead*), which translates more directly into "liberation in the intermediate state through hearing" and is read by a lama prior to death all the way through the next forty-nine days until the spirit reincarnates. Bardos are liminal states between an individual's birth, death, and rebirth. The text is read while the spirit can still hear, guiding it through the penumbra.

Learning about Death not only helps me prepare for Dad's but reminds me that Death is something I can and must practice. In fact, the yoga I have been studying so ardently and teaching all these years *is* the very practice of dying skillfully. As much as the honoring of Life as its own process: the mystical and gradual carving out and honing of consciousness. So that Death then becomes the ultimate experience of letting go, of releasing into the big bang when the time comes. And not only is it preparing me for Death with a capital D but for all the little deaths in between. I am training myself to abide. To withstand the bardo, the caesura, the space of loud silence and total emptiness that belongs neither here nor there, as well as everywhere. It is preparation for mastering my in-between-ness, the space of my transformation.

Draupadi

Queen Draupadi marries not one but *five* brothers—the King and the four Princes. Virtuous and beautiful, she is adored by all in her kingdom. The King has a gambling problem, but being a long-time yogi and student of "the self," he knows to wrangle this toxic habit through tapas—discipline.

The King's evil cousin, knowing this, plots to usurp the kingdom. Duryodhana visits the court with a set of magic dice tucked in his pocket. Suggesting they play a game, which the King declines decisively, explaining his addiction, the cousin feigns forgetfulness. After some time, though, the seed takes root and the King asks, despite himself, "Why don't we play with lentils like we did when we were children?"

So they play...

"Why don't we play for one rupee? One rupee is nothing!" the King begs after a few rounds, eyes sparkling.

One rupee turns into one hundred, turns into one thousand... turns into one hundred thousand....and well...on the story goes...

Until the King loses.

He loses everything. His wealth, his lands...even his crown with its jewels (chosen by his wisest adviser to amplify his greatest virtues).

The cousin jumps up with glee. "That's it! You've lost everything. There's nothing left!"

"Not everything!" the King answers defiantly.

"What's left then?"

"My Queen—Queen Draupadi."

The court gasps.

On they play.

One final round.

The King loses.

"Guards! Bring me Queen Draupadi!" Duryodhana yells.

The guards drag her into the Great Hall completely stunned. She's never been treated this way. She approaches the King humbly, asking, "My King, why am I being treated so?" The King sinks deeper into his cushion, embarrassed.

She approaches the Princes. "My Princes, how have I offended you to be treated so roughly?" The Princes stare at the floor.

"Your husband bet you in a game of dice and lost. And now, you are mine!" Duryodhana lunges at her, grabbing her sari (made of two pieces of cloth neatly folded in on themselves). He has only to pull but a little and the whole garment will come undone, leaving her naked in front of her whole court—a humiliation she will not survive.

Draupadi grabs his wrists to stop him, but he is much bigger than she. She realizes she has two choices: she can hold on, a struggle she will eventually lose, or she can throw her hands up into the air and ask for Krishna's help.

Throwing her hands up, she begins to pray, chanting a mala of Krishna's names, conjuring him, in a low, persistent monotone.

Sri Krishna Govinda
Hari Murari
He Nath Narayan
Vasudeva

Krishna, hearing the call, looks down from devaloka and sees Draupadi in distress. Emboldened, Draupadi's unwavering voice pierces the hall in its strident beauty, calling out—or rather, calling in...

He Govinda
Hari Murari
He Nath Narayan
Vasudeva

And with one final tug she begins to spin. A wild, glorious, whirling dervish. Heart and arms outstretched toward the heavens. Her singing turns into a wail. Her red and gold sari shimmering brilliantly in the light. A woman on fire. She keeps spinning and spinning, Krishna making her sari *infinite*.

Sometimes there is nothing left but to let go.

———

"So...Bug [*pant, pant*]! What've [*pant*] you [*pant, pant*] been up to?" Dad asks laboriously. His breath so short now he barely gets the words out. My heart pounds waiting to see what he will say next. My undiscussed letter hanging in the space between us. His eyes sparkle with mischief in the late afternoon glow, the way they always do when we're on the verge of one of our heart-to-hearts. Not sure if this is the moment we're heading into the mire, I follow his lead.

"I'm writing a memoir," I counter playfully.

We sally forth bravely into uncertain waters.

He gives me the same look he always has, a look reserved only for me. I know it and love it—love him for it.

"A memoir?" He looks me straight in the eye, adding in a low rumble, "And what do *you* have to write about?" For the first time ever our complicity lies completely bare, all cards out on the table. A timid new version of us—Father and Son—emerging on the spot, along with the irresistible urge to parry. He is more tender with me now than ever; his manner so sweet my eyes well up.

The week's been charged by Death's painfully serrated edges; a lens narrowed into sharp, unforgiving focus. I knew I had to tell him before coming home. I was running out of time. If I didn't, I would live to regret it. And there's no living where regret resides. He deserves a shot at knowing me. Really knowing who I am. In whatever time we have left. I owe him that much. Which is why I sent the letter.

His jagged breath keeps Time. Face flushed with pride and anticipation. I hold his gaze.

We burst out laughing.

Our laughter quickly turning into his gut-wrenching coughs. His lungs trying to escape the cavity of his chest somehow while his fists remain clenched tightly at his thighs. My heart cracks into further disrepair with every nasty heave. Oxygen tubes fly onto his forehead. When it finally recedes (after what feels like an eternity), I rush to pull them back into place and slide the blanket back over his legs. The compressor keeps working at maximum capacity, no longer able to supply the air he thirstily needs: a lifeline amidst constant, heavy panting in the tiny lungfuls that are still available to him.

Eyes bloodshot, voice thinned to a barely audible thread, he thanks me. I lean in, one arm draped over his slumped shoulder. The side of my head pressed up against his temple. I can feel the frail sliver of Life pulling away ever so slightly even as his shoulders relax a little, thinking to myself, "Touché, old man. Touché," relieved our shared sense of humor didn't kill him...this time.

This is going to hurt.

Roxy

My fascination with Death heightens my curiosity with what happens to the body after the spirit's departure. And as an anatomy geek, I wanted a more direct experience of what lies under the skin: the ins and outs of the physical body. When I see a post for a cadaver dissection course open to wellness professionals, led by one of the pioneers in the field of fascia, I jump at the chance to sign up. Ferguson and I set out for Tempe, Arizona, far away from our tiny Brooklyn apartment and our two tiny dogs, where I will enter the recesses of the human body.

Most dissections occur on embalmed bodies, making the cuts more arduous and time consuming due to chemicals thickening the tissue and dulling the scalpel. The bodies are also stiff from formaldehyde, not reacting like the body we know, making it hard to see how tissue moves. Fresh cadaver dissections, the kind I'll be doing, happen on *un*embalmed bodies, meaning the bodies are frozen for storage, then defrosted for the course. That's it. No chemicals, no preservatives. This leaves a four- to six-day window to peer inside and strip the body down before the tissue decomposes to the degree to which it is no longer useful. Not too many of these courses are available for alternative healers and those obsessed with the mysteries of movement and spark because bodies must be donated by their owners specifically for this purpose.

The morning of, I show up in my scrubs, ready to go. A pale guy with weirdly soft hands and a lab coat emblazoned "Master Dissector" waves us into his white laboratory, located next to Discount Gemstones in a generic strip mall. It takes me a second to land in the room. I'm nervous, having no idea how I'll react to a lifeless body at arm's length. It's not something one can prepare for: touching flesh, looking at it, smelling it. That morning, I'd almost lost my nerve, but Ferguson, not about to let me chicken out on her watch, gave me tepid encouragement before driving off with a promise she'd be waiting for me at the end of the day. I appreciated that.

My eyes wander to the long tables that are pushed up against the walls. It hits me. *They're here.* I can feel my heart pounding in my chest. I close my eyes to feel through the space energetically, a makeshift prayer. I want to ask their permission. Let them know they're in good hands (or at least respectful ones), that they are loved. Deeply loved in our shared humanity. Loved for having undergone the big chill. The Great Savasana. I try to sense if there's still some part of them lingering in the atmosphere.

The Ancients are here too. My constant companions.

Immense gratitude and reverence wash over me as I feel the way peace lives in death. How comforting. How surprising. My fear and anxiety dissipate.

Once unsheathed, a defrosted person-shape is revealed, not a clumsy pile of flesh and bones. The body is spirited, sensitive, graceful in death. A miraculous symphonic treasure map, an unflinching scribe, an elegant witness—patiently annotating every event, emotion, and shift—a most meticulous ledger.

Our group combines our knowledge to determine the biological sex—female—and cause of death—multiple sclerosis—of our cadaver. She has a colostomy bag, looks like she was in a wheelchair for a long time, is around fifty-three, and probably left-handed. Bestowing her with a name—Roxy—we're amazed at how her body acts so similar to life...*without* the life. How it moves freely, rigor mortis lasting only about eight hours after death. Beyond that, it relaxes, and it's uncanny how close to life Death seems. Roxy's hand, very much a hand with its fingers articulate in every way. Expressive beyond belief. Still moving in its wondrous spirals, cupping itself to mine in a most natural fit, fooling my eye and heart with clear signs of life where there are none. In this way, we offer her an odd sort of rebirth in Death as she graciously grants us a reincarnation of our own.

We track our discoveries on a board and add other clues as we go deeper. The more I look to narrow, name, and compartmentalize the parts of the body, the more I realize I need to do the opposite to extract meaning. We are a magic symphony of togetherness. No one part works alone. As I work on stripping Roxy's lifeless body layer by layer, all I can think is how magnificent *Life* is. Beyond the reach of our imagination. It's simply too miraculous to grasp, too indelible to dissect.

Labels, then, are only fit as the starting point for understanding. Mere coordinates unable to offer much detail in regards to the lay of the land. And no matter how much I aim to oversimplify—these parts, the complexities of the human herself, cannot exist contained within a label.

It makes me appreciate how each word we use houses a *suggestion* of a meaning, a distilled view with little nuance. How each name or nickname points to a slightly different aspect of ourselves: *Mila*, my nickname growing up; *Militis*, what Mom calls me to this day; *Litis*, made shorter for exponential tenderness; *Miu*, what Silvie called me; *Miles*, what Tía Vicks saw in me—which I then adopted.

Yet one name or word can feel all-encompassing, binding, limiting even: *Camila*. We can latch on to it, forgetting it is a marker, at best. We ascribe whole universes of emotional meaning, dreams, desires, aspirations to it. Who we want to be in the world, how we want the world to see us—and it all happens at the most intimate level. Words, names, grow roots in our hearts, just as we grow attached to our vision of what they are and who resides within them.

Camila or *Miles*.

Are they separate, or the same thing, or aspects of a thing? Do they all sum up to make a whole, or are they all perfectly accurate as is? Accuracy then becomes subjective. When I offer you my name or you offer me yours, it's an opportunity. Potential. We stand on opposite sides of a chasm, the only bridge between us—trust.

———

Dad gasps for air. I run in, knowing I can't help. But that's what you do. Leaning forward on his cane, defeated, he shakes his head and mouths the word "Doctor."

I run to the kitchen to get Mom. She calls the doctor while I help him with his shoes. Everything has to happen slowly and deliberately because he can't move fast. Which short-circuits my panic, because it's strange being forced to move so slowly when your world is on fire. It's late afternoon. We don't have much time before the office closes.

It rains in the afternoons in Bogotá, and today's rain is apocalyptic. We pile into the car: Dad wrapped in scarves and coats, his driver, Ángel (as old and grumpy as he is), Mom, me, and Dad's compressor, strapped into a seatbelt like a person.

When we hit gridlock rounding the corner to the doctor's office, Mom declares, "Fifteen minutes!" strain noticeable in her voice. The doctor's office is about to close.

I ask Dad if he can walk the twenty feet to the door. He shakes his head, eyes seriously bloodshot. "It's OK, I'll bring the doctor to you if I have to."

"Go see if there's a wheelchair!" Mom demands. I leap out of the car, storming the front desk, spouting, "Wheelchair!" The receptionist scowls at me, pointing at the corner lazily.

When I pull up to the car, soaked, Mom jumps out with an umbrella and the oxygen machine. We help Dad, coughing wildly, out of the car and into the chair and run him into the building.

We make it into the doctor's office. He stands to greet us, looking down at Dad choking in the chair, saying, "Hola, Carlos." When he shakes my hand, it's all over his face: this is it. We are out of options. He scribbles a prescription onto a pad. "Two to three drops, three times a day. More as needed. He will tell you." Ripping it off, he hands it to me. It reads:

Morfina.

"You'd better go. Filling this prescription will be hard this late in the day. Buena suerte."

Mom pushes Dad out, and the doctor stops me as I turn to go. "Camila, if you take him to the hospital, they'll have no choice but to intubate him, and he will spend his last breaths on a machine."

We had all agreed: there'd be no more hospitals. We pile back into the car, Tío Gus taking over for Ángel now, and set out to find morphine. Three pharmacies later, it is clear that we don't have the documentation required for them to release the bottle. I can't find any information online to make the process easier. We are desperate, and night has fallen. As we wait for Tío Gus at the last pharmacy, Dad says wistfully, "I think this is the last time I'll be out of the house."

I hold his hand as he looks out the fogged-up window. Mom is petrified in the back. The truth in his comment rings a little too loud against our hearts.

"¿Ey, viejo, did you ever in a million years think we'd be scouring the streets of Bogotá trying to get you a fix?"

He laughs, immediately choking. He's never done drugs. And I haven't learned not to make him laugh.

And it is...the last time.

Weezie

The day I turn forty, I stop giving a fuck. It happens suddenly. Overnight. Last night of thirty-nine: still giving a fuck. First morning of forty: zero fucks given. Just like that.

"How does it feel?" Weezie, my best friend, asks as I sit next to her, chai in hand. It's sunny on the dilapidated steps of the funky fisherman's cottage we rented in Delaware. Her fortieth is coming up in a month, so she wants to know. Overnight, a torrential downpour has flooded the street in front of the house.

"Well...I decided I'm gonna have top surgery."

"What's that?"

"I'm getting rid of my boobs."

It's the first time I say it out loud. The tone landing squarely at the center of the Truth gong. Hearing it, I know inside myself nothing is more certain or right. I smile broadly.

"Well, you've had them for forty years. Ya probably know by now whether ya want 'em or not." She shrugs and toasts my chai with her tea. "Cheers!"

Our feet dangle playfully in the river our street has become as we look out lazily at Ferguson and Abby splashing and pulling each other around in a giant unicorn floaty. A surge of joy like I haven't felt since I was a kid overtaking me.

———

Finding a therapist specializing in gender identity proves to be a real challenge. It's underwhelming and disheartening, but I need to talk to someone. Not having much luck, I see someone I know peripherally through yoga. During our first session, when I tell her my recent conclusion—that I am transgender—she says, "You're going to have to educate me here because I don't know much about what that means." Which makes me scream on the inside, "NO!" For the first time in my life I am seeking *help*. Years of fatigue crash down on me. I don't want to educate *you*. I can't. That's precisely why I'm here. I need someone to educate *me*. Someone who knows more about this than I do.

I thank her for her time and tell her it's not going to work. "It's not you, it's me" sort of thing. Then, desperate, I ask an ex who is a therapist if she knows someone. Which is how I end up in a dreary office in downtown Brooklyn with an even sadder little fellow lacking in imagination.

He listens to my concerns about ending up a monster, a troll, a pariah, my fear of people's reactions, my family being ashamed. He listens without complaint. He's not particularly helpful or bright, but in the end, he holds the space for me to figure the stuff out on my own, which *is* brilliance in its own way. Even so, talking it through out loud, I am finally able to see and verbalize how completely I misunderstood Raghu's teachings. The words.

I'm not the body
I'm not the mind
I'm something divine

I'm not sure how they were meant, but I know the way I absorbed them was not healthy for me.

Profound teachings leave space. The space itself acts as a teacher. But because we see the world as we are, not as it is, sometimes that space brings us right up against ourselves. Homophobia, transphobia, and feeling unmoored in the world for so many years didn't come cheap. They left solid impressions I've chipped away at for years, driving myself mad because I hadn't tended to the original wound. The one caused by the gigantic lie. The lie of *gender*.

The truth is that we all come into the world with the same parts. They're just organized differently. Therefore gender is a construct benefitting patriarchy, capitalism, and white supremacy. In untangling the knot that is me, I am beginning to understand that needing something for my health is not vanity or superfluous, no matter how much the government or anyone else says otherwise. It simply *is*. And it is OK. I can have sovereignty over my own body.

So as it turns out, the little man doesn't have to be brilliant. I also don't have to like him. He just has to fill out the forms—the thing I unknowingly came for. Fulfilling the government's requirement that a licensed professional agrees with me that I actually know myself. Sign on the dotted line, little man.

I'm certain our time is at an end when, after telling him I was assaulted as a teenager, he responds, "Not all men are bad." I just laugh, incredulous. No, little man. It's true. You're not *all* bad. But most of you could do way better.

It doesn't matter, anyhow. Deep down I knew where I was going when I stepped into his office. I hadn't come asking for permission.

The decision had been made. Permissions had already been granted where they mattered. And things will be laid bare one way or another. Even if it's taken a while to see what lies underneath it all. No matter the time, new beginnings cannot be shoved neatly back into the box from which they came. For the moment they are out, they've already outgrown the space they emerged from.

Ferguson

Having found a way to bolster my income through leading retreats—becoming a cross between adult camp counselor, travel agent, and life coach—I am finally able to carve out some time for myself. In September of 2017, after leading a retreat on a vineyard in Italy, Ferguson plans to continue traveling in Europe with her mother. When she asks if I want to join them, I know I won't. There is something I must do.

I take myself instead on a solo journey to Greece. My spirit, craving natural beauty, ocean breeze, and quiet. The moment I plop my backpack down on the hard bed of the tiny hotel in Athens, that little itch nags at my back. I look at myself in the mirror but see nothing.

I ease into my own circadian rhythm. My days, lackadaisical and unscheduled as I wander through narrow Athenian streets. Time moving differently in different places. Journeying into the labyrinth of the depths of my soul like the Greek hero Theseus, I follow my intuition—Ariadne's jeweled thread—from unknowing into knowingness.

This is my "Goodbye Boob Tour." And like most good things in life, I find Greece to be complicated. A hotbed of toxic masculinity, yet impassioned by all things *woman*. Opposition and dichotomy thrive here. The tension brings it to life. Complexity breeds its own kind of magic. When you find yourself squeezed from all sides, your rasa—your essence—is released, whether you want it to be or not.

None of this bothers me. It's precisely why I came, what I'm looking for.

When I travel with a partner, I am safer, cloaked in the beauty and grace of my counterpart. Her femininity protects me like a spell. People only dare go so far with a *her* around.

This time, I need to be on my own in a land so far from home that it's uncomfortable. Dangerous, even. A land where I don't speak the language. I need to feel what it is to be in the world at large without someone's love shielding me from its realness. I need to be unprotected in a heterosexist world; to be stared at and yelled at in bathrooms; to be scorned by men and women alike because they can't peg me; to feel completely unseen, a ghost without any kind of sexual traction or verve, a eunuch; to be noticed only as a curiosity, a circus freak. I *need* this. To experience it. Be completely submerged in it. Humbled by it. Obliterated and destroyed. Made so small there is nothing left of me. Nothing but what can't be killed. So I can see—and finally be. Distilled.

I am not the body
I am not the mind
I am something divine

Here, I understand. Finally. In my bones—the depths of my being-ness—that the me that is not the body, not the mind, that *is* divine is both my mythical self and my essence. I'd been so scared of who I am and how people would react to me. Scared of being abandoned. I had leaned on my fear like a cane—a danda. Now I'm ready to take that danda in my bare hands like the ancient sadhus of India and break it over my knee like a fucking Olympian!

I'd misread the signs, misinterpreted the learnings. *I misunderstood.* I caged myself within the very thing I loved most. And I don't need to do it any longer.

Here, I give myself over to the majesty of my own mythology and re-member, reconstruct, piece back together my own divinity. Here, I choose myself. For the first time. Choose Life. Without concern for anyone else. Release my umbilical cord along with everything else that is earthly. I *had* to learn to shape-shift throughout life to survive, to pass as a woman consistently for others. It came at a huge cost. Depleting my innate power and taxing my essential gift. This is my time to replenish, to heal.

To *heal.*

So I feel. All of it. The realness, the ugliness, contrasted with the beauteousness and the joy of knowing that even within the cruelty of this unfair and brutal world, I choose to be me.

I did my time. For forty fucking years I did my time. Living to not disturb. Shining my light through the sides of my prism instead of directly down its center. But I am done. I have reached the breaking point. Healing is underway. And it will not stop until I am whole. Wholehearted. Until I come home. To myself. Complete with all my humanity. I will no longer narrow, shorten, or flatten myself. Being myself is the only real thing left.

I begin to shed all the layers I piled on so carefully. Along with all of the hurt, all the pain. Leaving them behind like an uninhabited snake skin, an archaeological ruin of my former self for tourists to marvel over and take pictures of. It's all happening at a heightened velocity. Time ever changing and amorphous. All the layers melting away one by one. Revealing what has always been. Vulnerable. Exposed.

> *I come to Greece to find hauntingly beautiful, odd,*
> *single-standing doorways.*
> *Everywhere, doorways.*
> *Doorways on mountains, on top of random rocks*
> *and clearings.*
> *Doorways on beaches and embedded in the cliffs.*
> *Nothing but doors along with their frames.*
> *Standing alone.*
> *Always unlocked.*
>
> *All I must do—*
> *is walk through.*

And so it is here, in Santorini, on a gloriously beautiful, sunny September day, that I float in a hidden swimming hole of the most brilliant azure water I've ever seen. As I look up at a crystal-clear sky, I finally get out of my own way and experience the orgasmic unfurling of my wings. Spread to their full expansiveness around me. Iridescent. Magnificent in the sun.

It is here, in the weightlessness of my deep relief, swaddled in the ocean's womb, that I embrace my own brilliance. And nestled within the seat of my own power, I weep. Weep for all that is, all that could've been. Weep from fatigue and exhaustion. And weep for what's to come and all that will be. I weep with grief for the me that isn't. And tears of joy for that which is. Weep salt tears, no different than the ocean water that holds me. Peace soaks through to the lava marrow of my bones. Peace soaks through. And the whole while, in my ears, the underwater murmured hum of my true tongue returns—

So Hum

I

am

that

———

That afternoon, sunned and salted, I ride the beater moped I've rented along the Odyssean cliffs, howling into the wind. My wings spread across both lanes, drying in the warm summer breeze. Free at last, shimmering and gleaming in the golden light, casting their giant shadow—a portent—on the road ahead. Never have I felt so good. So real.

I stop on a deserted peak near Oia. Perched on the highest rock I can find, I look out over the glimmering Mediterranean. Yelling with all my might, the sun, the cliffs, and the Ancients as my witnesses, I swear an unapologetic farewell to my breasts, and Life, as I know it. My howling booms and bounces over the rocks, ricocheting on the water, sending the message over the distance to let my spirit know that I will *never* deny him again. Now there is no other way but through. Where the sun meets the ocean, here, at the end of my world, I stand, charge toward the edge, and push off with one foot as I extend the other leg out into the air. I jump—

Now I know.

    Now I know.

        Now I know.

            I remembered—

                you.

And somehow, here, amidst gods that were not my own,

                I flew.

———

"You look GAWGEOUS!" Ferguson exclaims, combing her fingers through my feathers. A magical creature herself, nothing in that realm fazes her. She's come to get me at the airport, and Arlo is so excited that he pees himself a little. The puppies don't seem to notice any difference, except for Arlo's complaints that I'm taking up too much space. On the drive home I tell Ferguson I will start looking for a doctor.

The next day I secure a consultation. "Oh, wow. You mean like, *now* now. OK. I forget you don't waste time once you've made up your mind," she says plainly. "Let's go!" She's known who I am. Always. She's seen me wrestle with the world the four years we've been together. She's wrestled with it some too.

Just a year before, we'd sat in the picturesque patio of our favorite little Mexican hole-in-the-wall in Brooklyn, when she started bawling inconsolably. She'd pulled her hand from mine twice on our ten-minute walk there. It was date night. I asked her what was wrong, even though I kind of knew. She kept saying over and over that she was afraid. She'd been saying that a lot the past few days. The horrifying massacre at the Pulse nightclub in Florida, where forty-nine queer people were killed and another fifty-three injured, had happened the week prior and we were still in shock.

I held her hand while she cried, wondering what was so different now? *Hadn't it always been scary to be us?* I mean, we got preyed on everywhere we went. We were like circus people: always on display. Sometimes it wasn't overt, but it was almost always there. We were even preyed on at a wedding *where I was the officiant*. And then, we were surrounded by friends. That's what it'd always been like for us. Every day was a conscious choice to walk tall. Holding hands, still a revolutionary act, an act of courage. Activism in action. Even *today*.

After bawling for a while, she slowly said it—what was bothering her. "If anyone

ever comes after us, I'm worried about my family."

"OK," I said, a pit forming in my stomach.

"If anything ever happens, I'm afraid for you." I knew where she was going with this.

"OK."

"It is *you* they will kill *first*." Even so, it hit me hard.

I smiled weakly, looking more like I might throw up. She was worried I wouldn't come home. What could I say? *She's right*. It's a liability to love someone like me. Many who have loved me deeply had opted out before her. I'm not for the faint of heart. If people aren't down with the gays, the queers, the weirdos, and queerdos, they certainly are even more terrified of the likes of me—a downright nonconformist transgender unicornio.

———

After waiting almost three hours to be seen by the surgeon I'd found through an NPR podcast, we're ushered into a very pink office without so much as an apology. I am handed a very pink robe. Ferguson sits in the corner, clutching my clothes tightly, biting her lip.

The doctor, in his seventies, comes in. Without hesitation or introduction, he opens the front of my very pink gown in his very pink office and grabs my very large breast along with its own pink nipple. He feels the shape, density, and size of it with his hand, then drops it like an udder without further ado. Plop. Making me feel very bovine. Ferguson's jaw is on the floor. I like pink, but there's so much of it that I should've known. Then he turns to her, misgendering me, speaking as if I'm not there.

"Why is she getting rid of her breasts anyway, they're not unappealing? I can do the surgery next Tuesday. She'll have a zigzag scar and no nipples."

"Wait!" I interject. "No nipples? No, that's not what I'm looking for." Panic in my voice. There's no point in having surgery if the projected outcome doesn't even come close to what I'm hoping for. Nipples are possible. The one other trans guy I know had a bad experience with his surgery, and *he* has nipples.

"Nope. I can't save your nipples. They'll die and there's no way to glue them back onto you. If you want the surgery, sign here. Leave a deposit at the front; the rest will be due the day of the surgery. Thanks for coming in, errrr...*Camilla!*" He says my name as if there's a double "L" in it making a "ya" sound: Camiya. Something people do that's always annoyed the fuck out of me. Nope, not my name. Not anyone's name, actually. Not a thing at all. A camilla is a stretcher—look it up, asshole. This is the straw that breaks the Camiya's back. "And not to worry, you'll walk out of here that very day."

Ferguson intercepts the stack of papers. "Actually, we are walking out of here right now. Thank you. Get dressed, babe, we're blowing this joint." I throw on my ratty old sports bra and T-shirt and we're out of there like fugitives.

Once in the car, I break down.

"It's OK, babe, he's not our doctor." She says gently, "Look at me. We're going to find someone who can do this and do it right." Then rants about how horrifying the experience was.

I listen and cry, staring quietly out the window.

"Why aren't you furious?" She hits the steering wheel with her hand.

The experience had unleashed some ancient PTSD, along with a lifetime of disappointment in doctors. After I'd cut my jaw from a spill I took off a horse at fourteen that left a long red scar on the right side of my face and paralyzed the muscles around my lips, I was sent to an electro-acupuncturist who shocked my jaw with electricity to try to get the nerves to fire again. On the third session, the doctor, a fossil of an old man, leaned over and stuck his tongue down my throat. I went limp on his table. When the session ended, I walked unsteadily out and told Mom he had kissed me. We said nothing more about it. We also never went back. That's how she could protect me then.

I hadn't had much access to the trans community other than through random Google searches. Horror stories of surgeries abounded online, with a wide variety of complications: blood clots, crazy scars, weird nipples, nipples turning black and dying, people being treated horribly before or after the procedure, you name it.

Having surgery already feels extreme to someone who barely takes Tylenol. Part of the reason I've not considered it till now. The truth is, I hadn't expected much from the breast surgeon. Being queer, transgender, and brought up as a woman had kicked all positive expectations out of me. I expected worse than nothing. That's why I wasn't furious. I didn't feel I was worthy or deserving of a nice outcome, not really, even though I was paying the same cold, hard cash as the next person. And I'm afraid that now that I've acknowledged this *need*, I will have to settle for something that promises a bad outcome because I know I won't be able to pack that part of myself up again and make it go away. I'm afraid I won't be able to live without it. It's too late for that.

The next day I call in sick to work. I can't bring myself to get out of bed. Ferguson leaves for an audition and I binge-watch all the TV and eat all the ice cream with the puppies curled around my negative space. My wings shriveled into nothing but a tall tale on my back. Greece feeling very far away.

But the day after that, my fight kicks in again. I won't be victimized. I can do better than that fucker. It's time to pool all my resources, shake the social media tree and whatever other tree is accessible to me, and get answers from real people. I email the trans men on Instagram who have nice-looking results. Only one person responds: Chris Mosier—the first trans man to be an Olympian—and oddly enough, the only one I follow. Other guys make me anxious. I can't relate to them. Their posts make my dysphoria worse. But I am inspired by Chris, his journey, and the way he walks through the world. It seems like we could be friends someday.

I'm totally floored by his kindness and humanity with me, a complete stranger. He gives me his doctor's name. He's soft with me in a moment I really need it. Says the surgery is the best decision he's ever made and he's not once regretted it. I know I won't either. He tells me the doctor is a specialist in this one surgery and the people in his office are professional and compassionate. They never misgendered or deadnamed him and they all believe strongly in their work. He had no complications, and recovery took only six weeks.

I speak with his surgeon the next day. He is an osteopath with a holistic outlook. This makes me feel better. The only bad reviews I read online are about his rough bedside manner. But on the phone, I find someone who knows what they're doing, precise and concise, who has thought everything through and made the information as accessible as possible for his patients. I'm after the mastery in his hands. I can bolster my bedside with people who love me.

After I get off the phone, Ferguson comes down the steps tentatively. *Well??*

"He's the one."

"Don't you want a second opinion?"

"I've got all the information I need. He's the one."

―――

Jamie, my cousin, comes to visit. We take a long walk in Central Park. I try to figure out how I'm going to tell him. It's a warm fall Saturday, and the city is lively with a wide spectrum of characters. We make it to a big strip where people skate and twirl Hula-Hoops.

"I'm amazing with the Hula," he says, grinning. "I bet you didn't know that."

He asks a girl nearby if he can borrow hers. Then pulls it over his head and starts doing a bunch of cool tricks. He's so sweaty and pleased with himself that we can't stop laughing.

Amidst the intimacy and softness that laughter brings I just blurt it out, "I'm getting top surgery."

No one really knows yet. I've been making a bulletproof case before telling people, not wanting their fear to poison me with doubt. I'm also tired of cross-referencing every decision. My decision is made. I'm only telling those closest to me. Everyone else will have to figure it out and get on board. It's a lot to manage everyone's feelings and expectations. It's also not my job.

"Oh my god! I'm SO HAPPY for you!" He hugs me. "CONGRATULATIONS!!"

It's the first time *ever* that I have received enthusiastic celebration about something that mattered this much to me. I'm so surprised by his outburst of positivity that I immediately start to ugly-cry.

"It's OK," he says, rubbing my back. "So, wait! How are you gonna choose your nipples?" I stop crying, confused by his question. "Because I'm thinking, if you want to keep them true to your genes, you could send the doctor a pic of these bad boys." He pulls his shirt up, proudly displaying his. "Ahhh? Waddaya think?"

We burst out laughing so hard that the line between laughing and crying is completely lost.

"OK, but seriously, you have to help me with something else," I tell him.

"What's that?"

"Telling my mom and dad."

His eyes go wide. "Oh shit!"

Ganesha

The sage Narada visits Shiva, offering him a magic mango that gives knowledge and wisdom to whoever eats it.

Shiva and Parvati have two sons: Muruga and Ganesha. Muruga is athletic and fast, his father's favorite. Ganesha is, well...a beast. An original. He has an elephant's head, a big potbelly, and is lazy, which makes his father crazy.

Not knowing who to give the mango to, Shiva tries making a game out of it.

"Boys, do you want to play a game?"

Muruga jumps up, excited. "Yes!"

Ganesha says nothing.

"OK! The first one to circle the world three times gets this mango."

Muruga jumps onto his peacock and rushes out the door.

Ganesha, whose ride is a mouse, lies on the floor, pondering his options. Slowly getting up, he walks to where Shiva and Parvati sit and begins to circle them. Once, twice, then a third time.

"What are you doing?" Shiva asks, irritated.

After the third round Ganesha stops, out of breath. *"You* are my world," he says.

Moved, Shiva replies, "You have made me proud. I am naming you Lord of all Lords. From this day forth, no journey shall begin without your blessing."

He hands Ganesha the mango.

Carlos

October, 2017
Subject: Importante. Por favor, lean.

Querida Familia,

Espero que esto los encuentre bien. I write with news.

As you may be aware by now, I've always felt like a boy inside my own skin. In psychology the term is "transgender." For the last while I've been working closely with a therapist, an expert in these matters, to figure out what the best course of action is for me personally. Through this I have decided on Monday Dec 27 to undertake "top surgery"—a double mastectomy. To that end, I've found an excellent surgeon who works out of Florida and specializes in this procedure.

I know this might shock you and be difficult to comprehend. I hope you can sense that I write you with joy in my heart, as this feels like the right decision for me. I am so looking forward to my outsides matching my insides.

The surgery is not as complicated as it sounds. It is outpatient. The recovery period is short and fairly simple. I will remain in Florida for a week for the post-op checkup and then head back to New

York. Ferguson and Todd will be with me the whole time. They are both on board and excited to help. I know you can't be with me due to Dad's illness and it is really OK. I will do great under their care. After that, we will head home and, depending on how I feel, start work the week after. Everything has been paid for and booked, and I am confident that the surgeon I have chosen is the best one for the job. I have been saving for years for this very moment.

Attached is the surgeon's website so you can check it out, as well as some articles written by a therapist who has a transgender child. I think they may be of help in offering some context. I also hope that if you have any questions, you will not hesitate to ask me. I hope this doesn't make you afraid of me. In fact, I am taking action because I believe in life we must always choose love over fear. So with this letter I am hoping to open the dialogue between us.

You know how much I love you. I imagine if you were to look back, this may not be the first time I've mentioned this. I've spent the last few years attempting to let you know how it feels to be me in the world. I hope you can understand that I have always been the same person. I also hope that our relationship keeps growing and getting stronger through this. Because I adore you. I must do this because my journey is my own. I must walk it with courage and grace and step into my truth. As well as the unknown.

Mil besitos,

Miles

———

On my third trip to India, this time as Raghu's assistant, while riding the infamous night train to Mathura, he tells me stories of his days as a straight-edge punk rocker in the '80s. His band is about to start touring Europe again, after a long hiatus. I mention how punk rock and slam dancing were big in Bogotá when I was growing up.

"Do you know Dag Nasty and the 7 Seconds?" I add.

"Yeah, I know Dag. He used to be my roommate."

"Really? I saw them live once."

"That's weird. I never pegged you for a punk rocker. Where?"

"Yeah, I'm not. Miami."

"No way!! My band opened that show!"

"No shit." I stand up. "I was THERE!"

"WOW! THAT show was *LEGENDARY*! Like, the show everyone still talks about! Punks would KILL to have been in your shoes."

"No shit!! Well...they would've been in very small shoes."

"What do you mean???"

"I was eight."

He is standing now too. "Wait. NO WAY!!! That was *you!?*" His eyes widen. Recognition piercing both our hearts. And before we know it, we're hooting and howling, jumping up and down, laughing. We've known each other for so long. Even longer than we thought. A brown arm reaches through the curtain of our bunk, pulling it wide, revealing a very cross lady who yells at us in Hindi to pipe the fuck down.

As we sit back down next to each other, elated, he turns to me and says, "You know, I thought you were a boy."

———

That's Dad's favorite story. It's unimaginable to him that one of the punk rockers from that crazy show thirty-plus years ago has reappeared in my life as my most beloved teacher and friend.

Back in Bogotá, when the doctor prescribes morphine, we all know the shadow is near.

I panic because my surgery is two weeks away. I can't sleep that night. Maybe I should change the date and lose the deposit. It feels like no plans should be made under the circumstances. This limbo. I am so congested emotionally I can't sense right action. I have to talk to my parents while we are still physically in the same place.

I know from their written responses to my letter that they're both doing their best to support me. Mom's response came almost instantly and struck a perfect tone. As if it'd been prewritten years ago and sitting in a drawer awaiting the right moment to be delivered. A true testament to the distance she's traveled from the days of deep denial. Her letter feels like a wish, a prayer for her future self to grow into, and even though I know she isn't quite there yet, and things are still very hard, I am so appreciative of her effort.

Dad's response, on the other hand, took a very long week to arrive. I didn't push him on it. I simply let it be what it would. Even though I started to get stressed with the passing of the days. He'd never taken time to respond to anything, so I knew how big a deal this was. His letter was cautious. Supportive in that he wanted me to be happy as who I am, but he was clear in stating that he thought surgery was a drastic measure, and that he was terrified for me.

We haven't talked about it yet. And though I'm nervous to face them, I also know Dad might have more insider information about the divine timing of things than I do. I need his help with this one. And I need to know Mom will be OK, whatever we decide.

I step into the office where they are puttering, screwing my courage to the sticking place. "I'd like your advice." They look up. "My surgery is in two weeks. Do you think I should cancel it or postpone it?"

Dead silence.

Dad speaks slowly. "No, honey. You [*pant*] should do [*pant pant*] it [*pant*] as planned [*cough cough cough*]." Which surprises me, considering his strong reservations about it. It seems like his thinking has evolved rather quickly in a short period of time.

I break down. "But you could die while it's happening."

"Well...if I die, I'll be dead [*pant pant*]." He smiles tenderly. "What difference [*pant*] does it make [*pant*] if it takes you a bit [*pant*] longer [*pant*] to get back [*pant pant cough cough cough*]? This is [*pant*] important [*pant*] for you [*cough*]."

"Mom?" Through my sobs, I look to her to see what she thinks. Usually, she defers to Dad on important matters, but this time she jumps in. "I agree. You need this surgery. Keep the date, no matter what happens."

I've never loved her more. I know how hard it is for her to say this. And I am floored by her bravery and love, even as her whole life is getting swept out from under her.

————

"Litis, it's happening! Your father can't breathe anymore. I'm calling the palliative care doctor." It's 7:27 a.m. I've just arrived back in New York. Mom is crying on the phone.

"OK, Mom. I'm on my way. Tell him I love him. I love you."

We hang up. I fall to my knees howling. Ferguson runs in to hold what is left of me. "It's happening," I bawl. "I'm not going to make it. I'm not going to get to see him off and say goodbye."

Pulling my chin up in her hand she says, "Do you think he can talk? Why don't you call him back? Say goodbye over the phone?"

She is brilliant. That hadn't occurred to me. *He is still alive.*

"Aló." I can hear the strain in Mom's voice.

"Mami. Soy yo. Do you think I can talk to him?"

"He's really short of breath, honey. He may not be able to respond, but he can hear you."

I hear his breathing, so labored, so short. "Papi. Soy yo. I've been the luckiest kid in the whole wide world to have you as a dad. You are the best dad anyone could ever have wanted. Don't wait for me. OK? Go when you need to. And don't worry. I'll take care of Mom and Susie. We're going to be OK. I will be with you from here the whole way. Safe passage, viejo, te amo."

"[*Pant*] I [*pant*] love [*pant*] you [*pant*], kiddo... [*cough, cough, cough*]," he whispers back. "I've [*pant*] been [*pant*] the luckiest [*pant pant*] dad." His voice trickles off.

The phone slips out of my hand. Relieved he won't suffer anymore.

Ferguson packs my bag and drives me to the airport, promising she'll join us as soon as possible. I call Susie from the gate. She's on her way with Santi, my beautiful teenage nephew, racing against time. Two hours, the stretch between Tunja and Bogotá, two hours too long. I know she won't make it either. I think she does too.

"What can we do?" she asks desperately.

The only path I know for this kind of thing is meditation and the only vehicle, sound. It's the only way I can think of to transcend the limitations of our skin to be with him.

"Do you want to chant with me?" I ask. "There's a beautiful Buddhist chant to help carry his spirit to the other side."

"Yes."

We start slowly as she learns the words with me. Combining forces.

Gate, gate, paragate, parasamgate, bodhi svaha

We grow quieter as the intensity builds.

Gate, gate, paragate, parasamgate, bodhi svaha

These words, used for what they are meant for, like a spell, begin to unleash their full magic. I feel porous, my skin dissolving. A loud calm taking me over as I persevere, while sitting at some random gate at JFK, murmuring to myself—

Gate, gate, paragate, parasamgate, bodhi svaha
Gate, gate, paragate, parasamgate, bodhi svaha
Gate, gate, paragate, parasamgate, bodhi svaha

Methodically we weave our love together through Time and Space, across continents, creating a net, a bridge, linking us all to each other, to Mom and Dad and to Lela, who passed a month ago. These ancient words, creating mysterious pathways through the subtle space between us. We travel toward one another.

As I see the matrix materialize from above, I mistakenly think we are building it with the mantra. Then to realize what one can only learn by being. We are actually uncovering what has always been. We are not alone. Never have been and never will be. We are bound to all others through our humanity. Joining everyone who has ever been here, and all those who will be. Everyone who has ever loved and mourned. We discover, through sound, the eternal bridge—the passage between worlds. The one we must all cross. A bridge beyond Time, radiant, made of thousands of bright, orange marigolds.

Gate, gate, paragate, parasamgate, bodhi svaha

Gate, gate, paragate, parasamgate, bodhi svaha

Gate, gate, paragate, parasamgate, bodhi svaha

Gate, gate, paragate, parasamgate, bodhi svaha

Gate, gate, paragate, parasamgate, bodhi svaha

Gate, gate, paragate, parasamgate, bodhi svaha

We stand together now on our side, that of the living, gazing across the way: Santi, Susie, Mom, and I. I feel you take your last breath—the first full breath you've taken in years. The breath of wonder as you see what's on the other shore. It is time. You look around at us and, with one last exhale, begin your journey home. This part of the trek is yours and yours alone.

Gate, gate, paragate, parasamgate, bodhi svaha

Gate, gate, paragate, parasamgate, bodhi svaha

Gate, gate, paragate, parasamgate, bodhi svaha

Gate, gate, paragate, parasamgate, bodhi svaha

Gate, gate, paragate, parasamgate, bodhi svaha

Gate, gate, paragate, parasamgate, bodhi svaha
Gate, gate, paragate, parasamgate, bodhi svaha
Gate, gate, paragate, parasamgate, bodhi svaha
Gate, gate, paragate, parasamgate, bodhi svaha
Gate, gate, paragate, parasamgate, bodhi svaha
Gate, gate, paragate, parasamgate, bodhi svaha
Gate, gate, paragate, parasamgate, bodhi svaha
Gate, gate, paragate, parasamgate, bodhi svaha
Gate, gate, paragate, parasamgate, bodhi svaha
Gate, gate, paragate, parasamgate, bodhi svaha
Gate, gate, paragate, parasamgate, bodhi svaha
Gate, gate, paragate, parasamgate, bodhi svaha
Gate, gate, paragate, parasamgate, bodhi svaha

With every step the bridge becomes visible under your feet. I can't see them with my eyes, but I know the Ancients are there, waiting patiently alongside your people on the other bank. I can feel them with my heart: your best friend Gary, Lela, Tía Cris, your mom, Marina, and dad, Ernesto, and all the others.

Gone, Gone, Beyond the Beyond,
All the Way to the Other Shore.
Awaken!

Exhausted, I cry myself to sleep. When I wake you are gone. And I am home.

I am afraid it will feel hollow. Life. Without you. Mom feels so tiny when I hug her at the door. The funeral home has already taken your body. Even so, the otherwise usually cold apartment feels warm with your spirit as I walk with trepidation to your room. Unsure of what I will find or what to expect. I stop in the doorway. The hospital bed and compressor, already gone. *You are here. Standing with me.* I tear up. Not because your stuff is gone. But because your Death is our Death as well as a new beginning for all of us.

Surprisingly, I am OK.

I am only able to see you the next morning through plexiglass. You look weird lying there, so close, yet the farthest you've ever been. Your hair, a little too long but beautiful, silvery white and full. Your skin, waxy. You look peaceful. I stand there for a long time making little tear puddles over you, sending you love. No one interrupts me. They leave me to my grief. I am grateful for that. Then the casket is sealed before visitors are allowed in.

This is the last time I see you.

There are so many people. Friends, family, farmhands, friends of Mom's, work mates, Susie's friends...many of them I remember, many I don't.

The handsome neighbor from across the street, Miguel, comes over, looking mighty dapper in a pin-striped suit, only a little younger than you. He offers me his condolences before turning to Ferguson. "You're a lucky woman to be in love with this guy." I'm taken aback by this irreverently kind gesture amidst the heartbreak. I haven't seen him since I was a teenager. I'm wearing a suit and a tie, not caring anymore what anyone thinks. I wanted to look my best to see you off, and for Mom. Even though you wouldn't have cared, I knew she did. "Hang in there, handsome." He puts his hand tenderly on my cheek and leaves, taking some of my tears with him.

Ferguson and I step out for fresh air. She arrived on the red-eye this morning. It's almost 3:00 p.m.—time to take you into the cathedral. They crank out the services in precise forty-five minute slots. I panic, run upstairs, afraid I'll miss my chance, dress shoes killing me from standing all day. A strange fear taking hold that I won't be allowed to walk your casket out because I am not a man.

Time slows as I step into the room.

There is a silent knowing, like when a horse dies.

No one speaks in the stifled air.

My uncles, out of character, look to me to lead.

I feel you here, behind me, and when they look at me, you walk
inside my skin. They are looking to you now.

I am a man. How strange.

When the veil thins, it thins in all directions.

Which is how I've fully phased over into this world.

As if dancing, we all move in synchronized steps to flank you. I don't know who is here, but I know it's whoever needs to be. Santi, Gus, Matt, Ángel...I am just happy no one tries to stop me. I would've turned wolf. I guess they know better than to mess with a broken man.

We wheel you into the ribs of the cathedral. It's not hard to find Mom. The bereaved get front row seats to such events. Mom doesn't participate in any of the prayers. She has a right to her rage, losing you and Lela within a month. Ferguson is the only one who takes Eucharist. We haven't eaten much today, and when she returns to the pew she looks at me mouthing, "I was hungry," making me smile.

An incredibly out of tune rendition of Leonard Cohen's *Hallelujah* in Spanish echoes through the chamber. I look up to see a bunch of very tired-looking cadets singing from the balcony. There's something ludicrous about it. I can't stop the giggles. My eyes catch Tía Betty's and I see she's giggling as well. By the end we all are. Everything is a shattered kind of perfection.

When service is over, the hearse takes you to the cemetery for cremation. When asked if she wants to go, Mom makes a resounding "Nooooooooo!" She is headed home.

"I'll go," I volunteer. It's all happening in real time. I want to walk you all the way. Breaking custom, Susie and a small group of us pile into a car and head back down the same dirt road that flooded way back when.

We wheel the plain pine box into the crematorium. The coffin's elegant outer shell has been removed by the undertaker. A woman stands by the doors to the oven and, seeing us, opens them. We can see the flames. We stop. Look around at each other: my two uncles, Santi, Susie, Ferguson, and I. We all touch the box and share a couple of stories, bidding you farewell. Then we walk you into the fire and the door closes.

This is the most beautiful part for me.

A few days later we are handed an earthy terra-cotta egg containing your ashes. We bury you under a tree and at the end of the ceremony, we are offered a large plastic green watering can with which to water the ground that covers you.

You would've gotten a kick out of that.

———

No one tells you that when someone dies, their qualities—the sum of who they are—transmute suddenly. In a burst, their energy must find a new home. You don't think you'll see those qualities ever again, only to turn around and see them manifesting without warning in those you've known your whole life. And then to see them exponentially more visible in yourself...it's a strange sort of reincarnation. A comforting one.

Susie

Ferguson returns to New York while I stay in Bogotá with Mom. There is much to be done. First off, helping Tía Vicks close out Papo and Lela's apartment, with Papo now in a home. Lela's death, a little over a month ago, was eclipsed by Dad's final days. The packing, suspended in time.

Terrified of death, Lela hadn't let doctors treat a wound on her leg and became septic, bringing her face-to-face with the very thing she feared most. And because she had declined medical intervention, the insurance company washed their hands of us. Mom and Tía Vicks, in a moment of pure panic, had the brilliant wherewithal to reach out to the foundation for dignified death started by Papo back in the day, pleading for help. They knew Lela wasn't going to go easy. She was a stubborn, complicated woman. The foundation thankfully came to their aid. Even so, it took Lela three whole nights to let go. True to herself until the end.

Sitting on Lela's bed in her half-empty room, my grief stops me in my tracks. I realize I've not yet begun to mourn her. In Spanish, mourning is el duelo—the duel. With whom, though? Yourself? A ghost? The past? Forgiveness? Death? I don't know. But I'm in it now.

It's unnerving to touch her things, never mind pack them without her consent. She was so particular. And here we are, going through them, deciding what has value and what to throw. But who are we to know? I miss her. I remember the many times I would offer her another rum when her glass was low, and she'd say, "No gracias, mijita...bueno, tal vez un poquito (well, maybe just a splash)." Indicating the tiniest amount with her fingers with a roguish grin.

Then, we have to go through our apartment. Donate all the outdated electronics Dad tucked away in every inch of closet space. Close out bank accounts and old phones, find passwords, and make sense of Dad's chicken-scribbled notes amidst piles of recipes he was finessing. We have to "take back" the TV and phones, which are booby-trapped with outdated pirated software none of us know how to use, so Mom can have access. And lastly, clear out his closet. That one's a bitch. I'm not gonna lie. Which ends in me kicking Tío Gus out, because he won't leave but also won't let us give anything away. He's not good with such things, keeping everything. He's still holding on to a bag of screw anchors Abuelito Ernesto purchased somewhere. And don't you dare suggest he get rid of them either. Screw anchors! Grief manifests in the strangest of ways. The work is as grueling as it is healing and takes the whole three weeks before my flying to Florida, of all places, with my only suit and dress shoes still in tow, for the second most significant moment of my life: top surgery.

This is also the longest break I've ever taken from teaching, and even if it breaks me financially, I don't care. I need it.

———

When Todd turned forty, I asked him, "What do you want to do for your birthday?" Long gone were the days of living together in New

York with Daphne. He was back in Salt Lake and had remembered his sense of humor. He had also landed a job as faculty in the same program we both graduated from back in the day at the University of Utah. When Dad died, Todd was the first of my friends to offer to be at my side for the funeral. Which meant the world to me.

At the time, Todd responded to my question with no hesitation, opening his arms and yelling, "Disneeeeeyyyy!!!" Caught off guard, and like the curmudgeon I've become, my knee-jerk response was a definitive, "NO."

So with two days in Florida to spare before the pre-surgery consult, I propose we treat ourselves to Disney World, because even though five years have passed, I still feel like an asshole. He's thrilled. And I, so broken that it doesn't matter where we are or what we do. My mood seesaws between extreme grief and overwhelming elation at all the things. While home, out of respect for my family's grief, I didn't speak of my hopes and fears regarding this life-changing surgery. In fact, I didn't speak of it at all. Though I know this will be one of the greatest things to ever happen to me, I'm also terrified of all that can go wrong, of people's worst fears being confirmed, and having to continue to defend my position. I know this surgery feels extreme to most everyone. So I don't think it fair to pile my stress about it onto their grief, and also don't want their fears harshing my fragile frame of mind. But the whole situation leaves me in a tusa.

Surrendering to the garishness and crowds at Disney seems as perfect as it is a ridiculous antidote under the circumstances. To make the stakes even higher, Hank, our Maltese, gets violently ill just as Ferguson is due to meet us, opening the possibility that she may not make it at all. Everything feels thick and devastating.

But when Todd and I ride Space Mountain and he screams like a ninny, I cackle the whole way down, feeling that my job here is done. And fortunately, Ferguson and Hank arrive right in the nick of time.

The day of the surgery we show up early to the small clinic. After a brief wait we are taken into the back, where the doctor draws a map of my body-to-be on my now-body, detailing the road to my new life. The anesthesiologist works his magic and as they wheel me out, I flash Ferguson a genuine, open smile. She's never seen me this happy—or so she tells me afterward, fighting off tears. I guess the more life pulls on that sari, the closer I get to my inner-most essence.

The days following are uncomfortable and nondescript. The surgical binder around my chest, so tight that it makes it hard to breathe. There are drains and other gnarly discomforts. But nothing can stop my joy. Not even the pain. Because no matter what, *they're gone*. Forever.

A week later as I await the unveiling, a kaleidoscope of butter-flies going nuts in my belly, I think about what this doctor has done for me—offer me back to myself. How incredible that is. Knowing I will never be able to thank him appropriately for what he's done. I think about how important having access to this procedure was for me after forty years. And I'm humbled by how fortunate I am to have received it. I really don't think I could have continued without it.

Finally, we are ready. I stand in front of the floor-length mirror and unbutton my shirt, still wrapped in my chrysalis of gauze and bandages. Everyone leans in. The Ancients, peeking from behind Ferguson and Todd. Collectively, we hold our breath.

The doctor unwraps my torso carefully, methodically. When the bandages are off, he stands aside. MY CHEST IS FLAT. It looks hor-rible, all stitched up, nipples black and caked with Neosporin. BUT MY CHEST IS FLAT. And...all I can see...is beauty. Beauty in his artistry. Beauty in the depth of my gratitude reflected in the mirror. Beauty in Ferguson's and Todd's complete awe at my reaction. I explode into tears. A giant weight lifted from my shoulders. Literally. If I could've donated my breasts to someone else, I gladly would have. They were beautiful. They just weren't meant for me. I am so relieved they are gone. We are all crying now. It is too much to bear. The looking. The seeing. This pincushion of a torso—the most me I could ever have imagined.

Forty years.
Forty years not my own.

From here on out:
Be true,
Live raw,
Exposed.

———

Six weeks post-surgery, I'm back in Bogotá.

Susie sizes me up at the door. "You look good."

It means a lot. Not just the compliment, but more the acknowledgment that change is happening. For Susie, this change has come hard.

In academia, she studied the die-hard feminism of the '70s with some of the radical lesbian activists who spearheaded the movement. Whose beliefs are consistent with the views of today's TERFs (trans-exclusionary radical feminists), making it seem to Susie like I was betraying my womanhood to become a man, and thus a soldier for the patriarchy. The enemy.

But I'm not abandoning my womanhood, rather, I'm *expanding* its container to allow for my masculinity. Maybe this makes me less of a woman, or more of a man, I don't know, but it doesn't make me any less of a feminist. If anything it makes me more of one. I am also not *becoming* a man. I am becoming *myself*. The gender *expression* of which might appear more masculine, but the gender *experience* of which is still TBD. And even if I am a man, feminism needs men and cannot succeed without us.

Susie's resistance rears its head one night at dinner when she complains flippantly, "The name Miles doesn't even translate well into Spanish. You should try Cami or Milo." (Milo—the name of a South American soft drink.) Without asking me about its origin, without even knowing that Miles had chosen me. Borreros have a way of telling each other what to do. Her words "you should" send me over the edge and I lash out, "Susie, it's not up to you!" She backs right off, staring at the floor.

For the last three years I've had to continually ask people to use he/him pronouns. A humbling ask, reminding me daily—and somewhat painfully—that I don't "pass" as male. Harder than not being *read* as male, though, is needing people to remember my pronouns. Not just once, but *every time* they refer to me. This feels like I'm making a big deal of myself and simultaneously asking too much from them. Especially when I'm not even sure they're the right pronouns. The only way to find out, though, is to experiment. And for that, I need others' help.

I wait until I'm sure before involving my family, trying to be as respectful as possible and do the least harm, and acknowledging that this is a huge transition for them as well. But when I finally ask, everyone just ignores me.

Except for Santi, my nephew. We've always been thick as thieves, and he's always known who I am. He finds a neat, innocuous way around my pronouns that is respectful even for others who find them jarring: he replaces the pronoun with my name. And that takes care of that! This blows my mind, and I adore it because pronouns feel like such a huge hurdle for so many, insurmountable even. Although, in my mind, they're the easiest gesture we can make that has an immediate impact on someone's well-being while exerting the smallest effort. All we have to do is watch what we say. We hold the power, with just words, to make someone, anyone, feel amazing—euphoric even, instead of like crap. And with Santi's method, you don't even have to use the damn pronouns! It's genius!

Then Susie calls one day. "Hey, can I get your thoughts on something?"

"What's up?"

"I'm having a hard time figuring out if this girl likes me."

Recently divorced after seventeen years married to a man who gives men a bad rap, she's starting dating women and is having a hard time reading the signs. And during our chat she calls me her brother. The first time she's ever said it.

"Wow. Thanks." I'm taken aback.

"The woman I've been hanging out with insisted I call you that because she says you are...my brother."

I quip back, "And thank the goddess you'll listen to *her*!"

"Well, it's just taken me some time to come to terms with your situation." She sounds hurt.

"Right. And that has hurt me."

Pause.

"It has?"

"Yes, Susie. While you were wrapping your brain around 'my situation,' I've been needing your support, feeling alone and scared. It's not about *you*. This is about me."

"Oh. Sorry. I never thought of it that way." She's crying now.

"I know. I guess I've always wanted you to love me as is. Without needing me to justify my choices. You may not agree with them, but I'm not even asking you to agree. I'm asking you to be in my corner because you respect and trust me and you know I have a good head on my shoulders. I've always supported what you've wanted to do or be. Even when I haven't fully understood it. That's all I've ever wanted in return."

"Oh."

But something clicks. She finally hears me. And starts putting in the work to meet me. That's really all anyone can ask of another—the willingness to try.

Monster

As in all transformations, things take time. They reveal themselves as you walk down the path.

I squeal in a friend's yoga class when he assists me in a supine twist, digging his thumb into my glutes. "Oh shit! That's tight," he says. "You're sitting on a decision you know you have to make but haven't." When I look at him like, *what the fuck?* he adds, "Or I'm just full of shit."

He isn't. There is. It's huge.

Testosterone.

But I've promised myself I won't make any decisions until I've lived at least one year in this new body.

And what a year it is.

When my friend Abby comes to visit, I'm so excited to show her my chest that I surprise us both by pulling my shirt up unexpectedly, exposing the hot pink smile etched across my torso (still open at the ends from the drains). Things are violently bundled and wrinkled and I guess I underestimated how butchered I still look, because she looks away in horror, having no idea it's been much worse. I should've given her fairer warning.

Pulling down my shirt quickly I ask self-consciously, "Too soon?" We laugh awkwardly. Not what either of us had hoped for. But there's ultimately something comedic and sweet about how wrong the moment goes. What is friendship, anyway, if you can't let a little weirdness live between you now and then and still love?

Then in February, while leading a retreat on the Colombian Pacific coast, I take my shirt off outdoors for the very first time. Mom is on the trip even though it's only two weeks after Papo's death. My scars are still fresh, so I keep them out of the sun by wearing a shirt. But on an overcast afternoon, with the silvery mystery of the Pacific calling and Mom nowhere in sight, I peel the last layer off, the wind on my skin, and run down the empty beach, diving into the bay.

I have waited my whole life for this.

Swimming out to a far rock with the warm water grazing my chest, tears of joy turn me into ocean. In the distance, I spot a school of dolphins. Opening my wings, I fly out to meet them, diving straight down into the water, twirling playfully at their side.

Later they escort my joy back to the beach.

———

That spring, on the way to Bhutan to lead a retreat that has been a year and a half in the making, I stop in Delhi where I treat myself to a Vedic chart reading. Searching for the exact time of my birth, I find two versions of my Brazilian birth certificate, each with a different time stamp, and another handful of Colombian ones with yet another one. I text Mom, "Are you sure I was born at 5:30? All my papers say something different." She texts me back, "I didn't look at the clock, honey, but that's what I remember."

And out of all the names, last names, birth dates, and gender markers I've had, this tiny (seemingly trifle of a) detail is the one that makes me feel unmoored. Nothing in my material life ever matches up. Once just to the left of legality, always just to the left of legality, I guess. When the astrologer starts in, "The placement of Mars in your chart complicates your gender," though, the audience is suddenly listening.

At the welcome museum in Paro, we are told that the Bhutanese mourn for forty-nine days. That's how long they believe it takes for the spirit to leave the body.

On the day of Papo's passing, Mom and Tía Vicks are with him, his favorite bambucos (a kind of Latin polka) playing softly on the radio ready to carry him toward the inevitable. Making headway on the sweater she's knitting, Tía muses, "Can you believe Mother passed thirty-nine days before Carlos, and Carlos thirty-nine days before today?"

"Whoa." Mom wrings her hands.

"Yup, I did the math." Tía nods, narrowing one eye to examine her latest stitch.

Mom flutters her lips, exhausted, sinking into her chair.

Later that evening, they dab a taste of aguardiente on his lips and whisper that his mother, whom he visited every afternoon in life to share a small shot of aguardiente with, is waiting for him.

Papo departs shortly thereafter.

It makes me wonder if Lela's bardo overlapped with Dad's those extra ten days on purpose, to show him the ropes, and if Dad did the same for Papo. Ten days to transform together. Leaving Papo for last because, out of all of them, he seemed to need the least help. He had swum easily in and out of his body for a long time.

This is something we shared, as well as an adventurous spirit. He'd spent a month in Antarctica at the age of seventy-six studying the polar ice caps with Uncle Nando, Mom's youngest brother. Giving me something to aspire to. He'd never made it to Bhutan but would've loved it here. The beautifully preserved forests. The colossal mountains. He was ninety-seven when he finally died.

Among other things we shared, Papo and I, was our bizarre name karma. Somewhere along the line, his last name had been changed by one letter on his ID—from Echeverry with a *y* to Echeverri with an *i*. The mix-up had gone unnoticed until Mom and Tía Vicks went to collect his ashes and the coroner shook his head adamantly, "No, señora, I can't give them to you." Tía Vicks, astonished, asked, "¿Pero cómo así?" He simply pointed to her ID, saying, "You're not family."

Luckily, a friend of cousin Javi's, Tía Vicks' son, had Papo's *second* last name—Parra—as his first. Javi called him up. "Parrita, can you do me a huge favor? I need you to pretend to be my grandfather's grandson so that we can collect his ashes. I'll buy you dinner? It'd mean a lot to my mom." Off they went to the cemetery, Papo finally landing in the rightful hands.

Looking through old passports later, we noticed that Papo had been an Echeverri, at least since 1934. Leading to yet another disturbing question: Was it *his* mistake? Or *ours*? Had he spawned a whole line of Echeverrys without meaning to?

I was surprised when Dad had asked, "Why Bhutan?" and it was Mom who chimed in, "Why not? It's the happiest country on Earth. Look at the gorgeous Royal Dragon family," showing him a picture of the king, queen, and their adorable little baby on her phone. Mom was most excited for this trip, even though she usually found my travels east a bit too exotic. But Bhutan fascinated her. What was the "happiness quotient," anyway?

On the trek I end up hiking next to our Bhutanese guide, a young man of twenty-seven, for part of the way. He shows me a picture of his sister on his phone and says, "You remind me of her." I look at her smiling face, wondering what we could possibly have in common. "She died," he tells me. Going on to explain how she was younger than him, gay, and with a girlfriend she was very attached to. They fought hard and loved hard. She also struggled with depression. Except that the Bhutanese don't have a word for that. There's also no word for gay or queer. Wow. Just because we can't name things doesn't mean they aren't there. *Does it?*

The couple had a huge fight a year ago, ending with his sister locking herself in her room. Calling her brother, who was hiking the same trek we're on now, she said goodbye. And before anyone could get to her, jumped out of a five-story window.

Hearing this, I want to explode into tears but know he chose me—a stranger—so that he can own his grief. So I simply listen. Life is full of such terrible heartaches sometimes.

His story stays with me. Not even living in the happiest country on Earth can offset the sadness of being queer in this world. Leaving me with much gratitude for never having to take that road myself.

For her and all others who have, I have a responsibility to live my life to the fullest.

———

That August, a Japanese yoga studio flies me to Tokyo to lead a teacher training. Once there, I am determined to visit an onsen, a bathhouse, before leaving. But thanks to the yakuza, the Japanese mob, tattoos are not allowed at most onsen. On my last day in Tokyo, the concierge pulls through, finding one that is more lenient. So I set off in the midst of a roaring downpour through the enormous Shinjuku Station to find it. Once found, I approach the front desk and point to my tattoos. The woman hands me two patches and a pink fob bracelet, then shows me a flyer with four outfits to choose from—two for women and two for men. This confuses me. *Aren't we bathing?* I point to an Aladdin-looking getup, thinking it's pretty cute. Alarmed, she whisks the fob from my wrist, switching it for a blue one. That's when it hits me. The fob is for *the locker room.* What the fuck was I thinking?

Now, I feel just fine with where I am in my evolution and don't have a problem being naked, but even though I'm living more like a man, it's pretty evident that I'm not one. And I've still never used the men's room, feeling more comfortable in women's bathrooms because even if they're rude or stare, chances are they won't murder me.

I could make a run for it. But I'd have to explain my exit, which, due to the language barrier, would be a lost cause. So I brace myself, grab the fob along with the clothing, and walk in. At least the Japanese are so non-confrontational that I'll never know what they think of me anyway.

I take the elevator to the baths, not having considered that they might also be segregated by gender. And much to my astonishment, drumroll please, they are. I had imagined myself bathing sweetly with a bunch of lovely elderly Japanese women and instead, I walk into the changing room...only to be spit back out just as quickly by the turnstile, mortified. The men in there are *naked.* I haven't seen this many penises well...ever. And though Japanese men have small frames, they are still much bigger than I am. I'm also the only Westerner. When the towel guy comes out to get me, assuming I'm lost, there's no getting out of it. I find a quiet corner, noticing some guys holding a small towel over their junk, and think, *I look like them, sort of...on top. If you disregard the bright red scar clear across my chest.* Maybe I can pull this off. I strip and, with a small towel over my junk, walk into the bathing area.

Showering comes first. There's a system. I sit. Yes, there's a seat, so I sit. And just as I start to shower, the towel guy comes at me looking distressed, speaking fast Japanese, the only word I can make out—passport. *I've been found out,* I think. Slinging a towel over my bottom half, I follow him. He indicates I dress, rushing me. With no time to towel off and because he's standing right there, I throw on the clothes they gave me. Taking me downstairs, still dripping, a lively discussion with the front desk ensues while I wonder if it is illegal to be transgender in Japan and whether they will throw me in prison or worse. This goes on long enough to give me an aneurysm.

After much back and forth, the only English-speaking lady approaches me, asking for my passport. I explain that it is at the hotel. *This is it,* I think, expecting the worst. But then she just asks me to buy more cover-ups for my tattoos. The ones I'd used hadn't covered them all the way. I stare at her, a sad, dripping Western Aladdin, looking for my wallet, which is obviously still upstairs. I showed her my tattoos when I came in. She *gave* me the cover-ups, so I assumed she knew they were too small. She adds apologetically, "It's OK. It doesn't have to be right now. Next time. Next time," padding the air with her hands.

No, it's not OK. Nothing is OK. Next time? Are you kidding me?
There's not gonna be a next time. My nerves are shot.

I bolt back to the changing room to grab my things and go. But then I make the mistake of walking past the door of the baths...

Fuck. I've made it this far. *I'm just gonna do it!*

I grab my little towel, strip, shower, and waste no time. In a swift, bold move I walk past all the men to the pool that's deserted out in the rain. Stepping in, I feel like a rebel, and it puts a smile on my face. My wings unfurl and I float in the embryonic waters, taking the first full breath since entering.

So Hum

My happiness turns to ecstasy. Nothing is more glorious than a hot bath, naked in the cold rain.

———

I never look back after top surgery. Once my breasts are gone, only relief lives in their place. Things feel correct inside my body. My back stops hurting. I can stand tall. My chest feels more open, no longer aching all the time. And I have a lot more energy. My body loves the change as much as I do. As if my breasts never should've been there to begin with. What's weird is that most people don't even notice a difference. So even though I feel really good, it's as if nothing has changed in my life at large, an unsettling dichotomy. Living this way is *almost* glorious enough.

Ferguson and I split up that fall. Five years in. She falls in love with another. That's not all there is to it, of course; it never is. In the end, we carved ourselves into corners we couldn't dig out of. A small part of me was also holding back on the next leg of my transition because even though I had no doubt she'd support me completely, I was aware it may not be what she'd signed up for. I've been so lucky to have so many wonderful people walk me a stretch of the way. Every single one of them making me possible. My gratitude and love for them is absolute. And I am also tired. Exhausted from the endlessness in becoming, becoming, and becoming. The countless deaths and rebirths. Ferguson was with me for such a trying part of the journey that it didn't feel fair to ask this of her.

With her gone, Life has so much space. So much quiet. I live alone for the first time. Dad and my grandparents are gone. Mom is far away and knows who I am now. At this point, my decision will have the least impact on others. I am free. To go through with it, or not. Free to be responsible only to myself. A rare gift. As I look out my window, a mythical dove flies onto the terrace and perches on the railing. I've never seen anything like it. White with red and blue accents...like an alebrije, a spirit animal. It stares right at me perfectly still for an eternity while I debate whether I'm imagining it. And just as suddenly it flies away. A visit. From Lela. I am certain of it.

It's hard to describe the in-betweenness of being. The bardo, the intermediate state. Being neither man nor woman, neither girl nor boy. Being the most invisible and most visible, simultaneously. Always on the fringes. An outlaw. As well as very much in the spotlight. Seen as dangerous and constantly in danger by nature of my existence. Simply for inhabiting the spaces outside the well-lit streets of comfort and labels. Human beings like knowing what to call things. It's fatiguing to inhabit a world with no words. But there's also something electrifying in it—the curiosity and wonder of having to light my own hand on fire in order to see the earth under my feet and discover what's actually there.

In this middle ground, I get to have a little of both, but I'm still *perceived* as a woman. And most of all, in this middle ground, I get to keep my voice. Intact. I can sing—con sentimiento.

But doubts also flood this space. What if no one ever loves me again? What if I finally turn myself into the monster society says I am? What if I turn into a disgusting wo/man, something neither here nor there, unrecognizable. And what if I never sing again?

Worries not entirely unfounded, since every time I've opened up to friends about my transition, their response falls somewhere along the lines of, "But you're not going to go on testosterone, are you? That's so [insert negative adjective here]." Blergh.

The thing is—I really want to. Go on testosterone. I long to see and feel whiskers on my face. To see my muscles lean and tone. For my shoulders to broaden. I wonder how it will feel to look in the mirror and see...well, me. Even if that means looking grotesque to everyone else. I want to pull the sari all the way to its nonexistent end. Get so close to the thing itself that it won't matter what's under there. In the same way that kissing brings us too close to one another to appreciate any flaws. Maybe zoomed way in, nothing looks disgusting. Maybe zoomed way in, nothing *looks* at all. Looking not being the thing.

I ask a couple of trans guys, "How did you decide to go on hormones?" Their responses are surprisingly similar: "It was a matter of life or death."

This doesn't help me. Cursed with an overly optimistic disposition, things in my life feel OK. If it were life or death, there'd be no decision to make. I'd have my answer. Sure, "passing" will make life easier and take some of the questioning out of people's faces and possibly some of the misgendering from their mouths. And it will definitely do wonders for my psyche. But I don't want to take hormones just to fit myself into the box marked "male." I also don't want to take them just to be more comfortable in the world, or make everybody else more comfortable around me. If yoga has taught me anything, it's that comfort is overrated and that the magic lies in discomfort—the unknown space. I don't even believe testosterone will make me male, per se. Though I know it will continue to unfold what I am—something *different*. An altogether *other* gender. If I go on testosterone, I want to do it only because it is what is in my dharma. Because it is my next step. This is *my* journey.

But what of my voice? Something always has to be sacrificed in epic tales. Is this my sacrifice? This elemental part of my being? To add to this pressure cooker, my voice is part of how I make my living. Chanting, both in class and in communal kirtan, has been my signature and a big draw for my students. On hormones, I'll go through puberty...again. And the one thing I can count on is that my voice *will* change.

"It's not like you'll go tone deaf all of a sudden," Ferguson pointed out once. "It'll be different, but you'll be able to sing. It'll probably just take some time. You'll be turning yourself from a boy soprano into...I don't know...a tenor?"

Her confidence gave me heart.

The open space makes me bold. Hungry to have my feathers ruffled, I get on a dating app, presenting as a trans man for the first time. I strike up a conversation with a sassy Italian ex-addict. We have dinner. She makes it clear she wants me to take her home. I can feel her desire. She likes this. Me. What I am. I turn her on. She treats me seriously, rides me like a cowgirl, like I am very real. I don't scare her, though in the end she's scared of herself. It only lasts a few days. But whoa, I

Remember....

Maybe if this road leads me to become a non-singing behemoth, it'll still be OK. There are people who find even the monstrous sexy, worthy of love.

Walking back from a client's house on a crisp fall morning, the knot inside my head finally—miraculously—untangles. As I think about Dad and how calm he was in the face of his own Death. When I asked him about it, he said, "Honey, I have no regrets. I've lived a full, sweet life. I'm ready." He wasn't giving up; he was simply stating the facts. With his words in my heart, I realize the answer has been with me all along. If I die today—without walking myself *all the way* home—I will regret it. And regrets are products of fear. Fear that keeps you small. Of the unknown, of life and what it has in store. Was it fear that made Abuelita Marina close up shop? The opposite of regret, then, must be courage. Leaning into love.

With this clarity, I take off running down Fifth Avenue and, spreading my wings against the sky, I fly. The time is now.

I let the wind carry me, close to the sun like Icarus, knowing it won't burn me. Not today. Today, I burn hotter than it does. Over the city I fly, past Queens, out to Long Island where I see the two long fingers of land I'm looking for. There she is—Fire Island—one of my favorite places in the world. I land softly on the empty dock. With no one in sight, I lie on the still-warm wood, homesick for myself. Comforted by the sound of the water beating rhythmically against the pilings.

I have so loved the process of allowing my mythical self to come forth. It has been the greatest gift. I know, however, that it is time to let the chimera go. I have to give space now for the myth to fully materialize, to let the last bit of magic slip away, surrender it—to become whole. To break what is left of the danda and let even my voice be what it will. As the sun's warmth envelops me, I fall asleep swaddled in my wings.

The crisp afternoon breeze wakes me. Stripping off all my clothes, I jump in the ocean—the place I am from.

Down I go,
to depth of the sea,
the depth of me.

Take them back! I yell

The sound remains
Unstruck
Silent

I surrender them

And through the salty darkness
The answer rings thick in my ears

So Hum

Back I swim, to the dock, the firmament streaked in neons and golds. I dress, my clothes still piled there as the last ferry approaches. Walking up to the ticket booth, I buy a pass. The girl takes my cash and hands me the ticket, perplexed.

"You forgot something." She points to the dock behind me, where my abandoned wings lie drying, glistening with majesty.

"I don't need them anymore. Thanks so much." I nod without looking back.

As I walk to the ferry, I feel them catch fire. The illusion, finally gone.

A loud bark stops me in my tracks. I turn to see a rust-colored wolf taking shape from the smoke. It takes a galloping sprint toward me. I hold my hands out to stop the visage, but it's real. Jumping into my arms, it surprises me, licking my face ferociously, small enough now that I can carry him. Looking down, I know the ocean has sent me this one last parting token to get me through the rest of the journey. Embracing this tiny wolf tightly in my arms, heart beating next to mine, I whisper a sincere thank-you to Oshun as the ferry leaves the dock—knowing we will be together always.

———

Daphne and I meet up in Boston, at a little Mexican joint reminiscent of our Berkeley days. It's the day after my first testosterone shot. We haven't seen each other in sixteen years. And I am devastated.

Instead of feeling light, all I feel is the weight of my decision to go on hormones. Almost chickening out of giving myself the first shot, I called someone I had been on a few dates with, who got really feisty— "You can do this! Stop being a pussy! This is for your health!"—and it was strangely what I needed, so I impaled my leg with such terror and force that my thigh is still throbbing. I'm all over the place, raw with emotion.

Extremely pregnant with her first child, Daphne glows. She's wanted a baby as long as I've known her. It stings a little, knowing they aren't mine. But it also feels right.

It's as if not a day has gone by. Once you know someone like that, you never really unknow them. Though my heart has moved on many times over, our love remains, unperturbed by Time.

Our conversation goes right to the quick: amends, family, deaths...pregnancy. She tells me they aren't revealing the baby's biological sex. A sweet nod to me, I think. Then she asks, "Would you like to know it? You're the one person I want to tell."

"Of course!" I light up.

Hearing it, I realize there's a burning question inside of me. After thanking her, I say gingerly, "Can I ask you something? Have you always known...about me?"

A deep sadness wells in her eyes.

"I've only ever wanted you to find peace within it."

She sits with me quietly while I hold my head and cry inconsolably. Not entirely tears of sadness.

Tío

"Why does it have to be so public?" my not ill-intentioned cousin Juana asks Susie at a family gathering, referring to my transition.

February 1, 2020, marks one year. One year on testosterone. One year of recognizing myself in the deepest way I've ever known. One glorious, amazing year where life and everything around it have felt possible, robust. One year of living as a civilian. No magic. No wings, no cane to lean on...no voice. Just me and my Bowie—my wolf. As is. One year of fully, and I do mean fully, leaning into love. No amount of naysayers, stares, ignorant questions, misgendering, deadnaming, or uncomfortable encounters in bathrooms have dampened the profundity or joy in my experience.

In March, I visit Jamie in California. Wanting a child and not having a life partner, he does something unusual for men in our culture—something women do all the time. He has a baby on his own. Well, not entirely. But he takes the journey by himself into single fatherhood. And out of that effort, Tucker is born. I fly to the Bay Area to meet him.

While there, news arrives that Tío Ricardo is dying.

Life has serendipitously brought me to him at this very moment. How poignant. Jamie and I drive over the gridlocked Bay Bridge, Tuck napping in the back, to go visit Tío at the hospital. A risky excursion sure to end up in Tuck's tears, if not my own.

On the way, I get nervous. I know Tío would love to see me and feel in my gut that coming is the right action. Not knowing what state I'll find him in, though, I worry he won't recognize me. I've started looking a little different now. My voice has also just dropped. Part of me hopes he'll know who I am. But I worry I might look different enough that if he doesn't, it will make him feel crazy. Which will break my heart. The urgency of the situation leaves no time for fear. So love it is. And up I go in the elevator to the cardiac floor.

Hesitating in front of his door I hear, "Camila?!" It's my cousin Miguel, who lived with me at Tío's many moons ago. My heart overflows to see him, so many years have passed. He lives in Mexico now. Bad news sure travels fast, far, and wide.

An insatiable caregiver, not only had Tío taken us both in, but he'd always housed a random assortment of cousins, aunts, sisters, and family members, along with some of our girlfriends and pets. I always worried he would die alone, since we had all just been passing by, but Miguel isn't the only one here. The cavalry has come to see him off. I get emotional seeing them all.

When Tío sees me, it takes him a second. He stares hard. Thankfully he isn't fooled by my sorry excuse for facial hair. Mostly, I think he's shocked to see me in San Francisco. But, just as I'd hoped, there it is, the spark of deep recognition.

"Camila!! Gwad a ju doin' he'ar, Chuga Bowl?"

He lights up like the Christmas tree that stands forever festive in the corner of the crazy room at his house. How I love him! This sweet, gentle giant. I notice his long legs sticking out the bottom of his hospital gown. I'd only ever seen him in overalls.

"Tío! Where have you been hiding these gorgeous gams all these years? I never knew you had such nice legs!"

"Ay, honey! Gwans a diva, olgways a diva!" He laughs a loud, hearty laugh that ends in him grabbing his chest. Contrary to Dad's cough, I can hear his lungs drowning with water.

The Time continuum folds in on itself once more, perfect and bittersweet. He's always loved me, really loved me, as is. Loved me because I was the woman he would've wanted to be: smart, irreverent, with a hint of pizzazz. He loved me because I was the daughter he never had. His love goes beyond a father's love because he never had the option of having kids. I love him because he represents everything I want to be: abundant, loving, living life shamelessly, paving his way—a true artist. An original. Being with him, I am touched by how meaningful it is that someone appreciated the woman I was. It almost makes the effort worthwhile.

I lean down, put my head on his wide chest, careful not to squeeze any of the tubes. He is soft and still very much alive. I hug him hard, listening to his heartbeat, and melt into him, crying. He holds me a long time. The strange contradiction of the dying consoling the living that sometimes comes with death. Tears stream down my face. I pull my mouth up to his ear and whisper, "I love you so much. Thank you for being a father to me. Danny's gonna be so happy to see you. Give him a hug from me, and tell Dad I miss him."

"I luv ju tu, Chuga Bowl." His voice quivers.

I pull back, looking into his eyes one last time before kissing his forehead. Then I turn around and leave.

On the way back to Jamie's, I cry. Cry in gratitude for everything Tío is and all the love he's shown me. Cry that Life let me see him one last time. Cry because I won't be there to hold his hand when he departs and because I was here to hold it now. Cry at how beautiful and intact his sense of humor is, even under such duress. Cry, hoping I will be brave like that when my time comes.

I imagine many people in his life felt the same as cousin Juana: Why did it have to be so public? Why did he have to be so flamboyant? Why did he have to live so openly with Danny? Why couldn't he just tone it down, keep it behind closed doors?

When I met Tío, I'd just started figuring out who I was. Had I not had someone love me unconditionally, perhaps my story would've ended differently.

Two weeks later, while in a boat headed toward the Colombian mainland with the sun and wind on my face, Tío visits me. And I know. He is on his way. I chant under my breath:

Gate, gate, paragate, parasamgate, bodhi svaha
Gate, gate, paragate, parasamgate, bodhi svaha
Gate, gate, paragate, parasamgate, bodhi svaha
Gate, gate, paragate, parasamgate, bodhi svaha
Gate, gate, paragate, parasamgate, bodhi svaha
Gate, gate, paragate, parasamgate, bodhi svaha
Gate, gate, paragate, parasamgate, bodhi svaha
Gate, gate, paragate, parasamgate, bodhi svaha
Gate, gate, paragate, parasamgate, bodhi svaha

All the way to the shore.

I arrive in New York to learn what I already know. The lumbering queer Colombian Viking has plunged into the depths of the golden curtain toward Valhalla.

Tío is gone.

So much death has surrounded me these last few years, including my own. So much grief. It is a good time for him to go, though. He is leaving me whole.

Camilo

At the beginning of the pandemic, Mom was worried about getting enough exercise. I offered to start teaching Zoom yoga classes for her and her friends three times a week.

Then, in December of 2020, I spend a month in Bogotá with her. Knowing she always keeps a list of things that need fixing around the house, I ask what needs to be done. She tells me the new oven is a lemon, that the rack falls with just the weight of a flan and that though technicians have come several times, they haven't been able to fix it. Concerned about how dangerous it is, I ask if I can take a look. I notice the frame of the oven hasn't been properly screwed in. Finding a screw in the back that is about the right size, I secure it. When she tries to press the rack down now, it stays put.

She stands in the center of the kitchen baffled, eyeing me with wonder, saying, "I can't believe you just fixed that. They've come from the shop like five times and no one figured out what was happening."

I blush. "You know I've always spoken machine."

It's as if all the pieces of who I've been are starting to come together for her. The Timeline overlapping now in my favor. Dad's death and the loss of her parents, coupled with my transformation, had caused a crippling grief to overtake her. Her whole life was turned upside down within three months. I can imagine, from my own experience, how hard and scary this has been for her and have tried to show up and support her in the ways I could from afar. We've always been great pals, but I had started to wonder whether this new, emptier feeling between us was the cost of my choice, or her grief, or both.

But what began as a way to keep my elders limber—our regular Zoom yoga classes—has had a shocking outcome over time. It's as if Mom has started to remember herself, her joy. And remember me, who I've always been. She seems to be enjoying me again. Being together in person for the first time in many months, I'm learning that the emptiness I felt was less about my choice than a side effect of not being in the same place, of not being able to transition *together*.

The day after I arrive in Bogotá, racing against bureaucracy, knowing that Colombian offices shut down from Christmas until February, I rush to the notary to initiate the process of legally changing my name and gender.

That same day marks three years since Dad's death. Mom helps me gather the papers in a surprisingly sunny mood. Colombia doesn't require a doctor's note. At least it's refreshing to go in knowing my sanity isn't in question.

With a mask and a tube of antibacterial gel, I head downtown to be there right as they open. The security guard makes me walk over a wet mat to disinfect my shoes, checks my temperature, sanitizes my hands, and sprays me down with alcohol. I'm disinfected.

And there, in the practically empty clerk's office, I fill out the papers.

Current name: *Camila Borrero*

New name: *Camilo Borrero*

It turns out Susie was right. *Miles* doesn't translate well into Spanish. And while my name remains Miles in the mouths of those who know me, the most seamless transition for my legal name, in the end, is just the one letter. It feels good. A nod to the name my parents chose, as well as the one letter that shifted in Papo's last name. And I like the way it sounds when I say it. There's a maturity in it.

Ferrying the papers back and forth between the first and second floors of the colonial house while documents are typed, stamped, and signed, everything feels unexpectedly easy. I'd braced myself for the worst but to my great relief, one of the clerks knows how to do it and is happily helping me. After a couple of hours, she calls me to her window. "Don Camilo, here are your papers!"

Elated, I bat my eyelashes and flash my winning smile. In the twenty-four hours I've been in Colombia, I've been called "young man," "knight," "sir," "mister," and "friend," but this "don" takes the cake. "Mil gracias, señorita. I'm so grateful for your help."

On the walk to Susie's, the wind picks up. The reflection in a window stops me suddenly. Rarely have I looked at myself during the pandemic. There's been no reason to. My heart skips a beat. A young version of my dad stares back at me. Disarming me. How I miss him. My bushy hair, glasses, and smile make me look so much like him. It feels exhilarating and unfamiliar—looking at this stranger who is *me*, a vision revealing that which has always been.

Then I feel him. Standing behind me. Looking at me through his eyes, which are now mine. The overlap of him and me, alive. Past meeting present meeting future. Just like at his funeral when he stepped into me—igniting the part of me that was him from within.

So much has changed since then. My appearance being the least of it. And that alone is no small miracle.

I turn to go, clutching my new document hard against my now flat chest—delicate proof from the outer world that I am finally, at forty-three, phasing into being, materializing. I start to run, leaping and kicking down the street. Hooting and hollering, endlessly grateful and intensely euphoric to be alive, unmasked, completely and unequivocally me.

When I finally return to Mom's that evening, she is watching reruns of an old novela we'd seen together when it first aired in the '80s. During the commercial break she asks me cheerily to tell her everything. When I'm done, she sits on her hands quietly for a moment, then smiles innocently. "I'm amazed that on this day, the same day we commemorate your dad's death, we are also able to celebrate the birth of your life as it should have always been."

My breath catches in my middle, not sure how we got here.

I don't even try to hold back the tears.

Acknowledgments

As someone whose art was sharpened and shaped in the the-ater, I'd imagined writing, in contrast, to be a solitary practice. However, the experience of creating this book, from its inception, has redefined that into a wild journey of collaboration. To even *begin* putting words to paper, I conjured all the generous, mystical spirits who have nudged me along my path. Some, my closest people to this day, some complete strangers; some mentioned in these pages in the gems that ended up weaving this particular web, others, supporting from the margins but no less important. Then, to my surprise, my ancestors crowded around me, enthusiastically coming to my aid, becoming my ultimate companions along the way.

So to say that writing happens in a vacuum...nothing could be further from my experience. It happens in the phrases and para-graphs read and reread out loud to my patient dog Bowie until the musicality hummed. In the millions of little interactions, con-versations, movies, books, podcasts, and moments of meditative scavenging through the world—words, thoughts, and ideas catch-ing in my mind—percolating, incubating, and consolidating. And it even happens past the completion of the manuscript when it is emboldened, distilled, and brought into material form as an object of beauty and wonder.

I should then thank everyone I have ever met and everyone who has come before me in my family, for this book is a great synthesis of my life's work to this moment. I must also thank my friends, past and present, because without them none of these *aha* moments would have been possible. *I* would not have been possible. And, like any good yoga book, which this both is and isn't, I must thank my teachers for furnishing me with the tools to navigate the wild, turbulent waters of my life with humor and some semblance of grace.

I also must thank all my loves, those reimagined in these pages—and those who may not see themselves represented—for they have shaped me and been instrumental in helping me carve out a space for myself in the world.

To Raghunath Cappo, my heart's teacher, you are a constant source of generosity and inspiration in my life, the truest of mentors. To Shana Swanson, incredible yoga teacher, mother, colleague, and friend, thank you for looking out for me professionally during the pandemic and being the link to Liza, Ginger, and eventually, Gretchen.

To my family, I am deeply grateful that you allowed me to reimagine you in these pages as figments of my memory and perceived experience. To my grandparents, your true effect on me, I was unable to name in its fullness before sitting down to write these pages. To Tío Ricardo, thank you for your infectious laughter and the overabundance of love you showed me when I was lost at sea. To Dad, your laugh goes with me everywhere. This is a love song to you and Mom. And I know you are getting a kick out of all of this. To Mom, your strength, tenacity, wild streak, and adventurous spirit have been my greatest teachers. You have always known what matters most and allowed for growth wherever necessary, never ceasing to amaze me. To Julie, thank you for your unflinching friendship and for taking over the difficult role of becoming our family's beating heart in Dad's absence. And to Fede, you have reincarnated some of Papo's gentleness, excellent listening, and curiosity. Your presence in our family has brought immeasurable joy, tenderness, and a much-needed fresh perspective. You are all my world. Your unconditional love has furnished me with the strong sense of self, worth, and belonging without which I neither would have made it this far nor known my own magic. And without which I certainly would not have written these pages.

To the team of wickedly talented people who read the manuscript in its various incarnations, gleaned its potential, and acted as doulas. To Juliana Borrero, my remarkable sister, author and performance artist, you were first to read the manuscript and offer a path for turning my blubber into a real story. To Jamie Hunt and Seth Thomas Pietras for starting me on the process of publishing. To Elizabeth Raetz and Amanda Saunders, the best friends a person could ask for, thank you for not only reading the pages, but helping me keep my energy up throughout the process. To Jonathan Ambar and Dallas Andrew Graham for your detailed reads and offering yourselves up for conversations helping me refine my viewpoint and voice as a writer, and also for getting creative with me on ways to share it with the world. To my amazing friend and student Timmie Elsner for connecting me with the masterful Laird Gallagher—you are, indeed, still a witch.

To Denise Hopkins, brilliant editor and longtime yogi and friend, thank you for taking time out of your very busy editing post to offer some of the most succinct yet crucial feedback, which I believe single-handedly turned me into a writer overnight. Thank you for believing in me so deeply and extending your valuable connections without hesitation.

To Laird Gallagher, my unending gratitude. You generously offered your time and expertise to Sarah and me, listened and problem-solved patiently on Zoom, through COVID and coughs, in order to make the story gripping and give it a pulse. Your keen eye, brilliant suggestions, and open-ended questions were the essential ingredients that brought the manuscript to its final form.

To Nick Whitney from Feminist Press, thank you for being the first to want to publish this work. You unknowingly created an avenue to get us to this very moment.

Now for the dream team. To Liza Fleising and Ginger Harris, my agents, thank you for having a sense of humor, being patient with my ignorance of the publishing world, and being the incredible catalysts for this work to see the light. You've taken such great care of us.

To Milo Rubin, our youngest, thanks for the awesome doodles on my picture, bruh, they're gas. To Caroline Duncan, thank you for being with me through my dad's passing and knowing me well enough to capture my lovely author photo. To Howard Grossman, the artistic director of our cover, you came in with no time to spare and are such a joy to work with. Thank you for lending your vast design expertise and turning our inconsistent ideas into the striking face of our story. To Madeline Sturgeon, our managing editor, your patience is truly endless, thank you. And to all the incredible people at Regalo Press who have taken great care with our story. In a harsh world, you have been a breath of fresh air.

To Gretchen Young, our exceptional editor. We are beshert. Working with you has been a true honor and the manifestation of the wildest version of our dream for this book. The fact that we get to donate some of the proceeds to an excellent cause through your imprint only makes things that much sweeter. Thank you for your incandescent sparkle and for taking a gamble on this first-time writer. I am still in awe at the mysterious way life brought us together—worthy of a short story. Thank you for putting the finishing touches on everything to make it gorgeous.

And finally, to Sarah, my sweetheart, partner extraordinaire, and the official driver to my get-away Subaru. Babe, not only have you edited this manuscript in its entirety from the beginning, but you have ushered it, and me, through every point of the process to becoming a book. You have been the glue, the sounding board, the organizer of chaos, an incredible advocate, and my most patient love! Thank you for your faith in me, your inexhaustible, steady presence, hard work, and brilliant problem-solving. This soulful piece of writing belongs to both of us. It is your care and exquisite hand that has helped me bring it to light. I'm thrilled beyond belief that after everything, I still get to come home to you, our boys, and our puppers.

If I have forgotten anyone, please forgive me. It is rather overwhelming to even be in the position of being able to thank you.